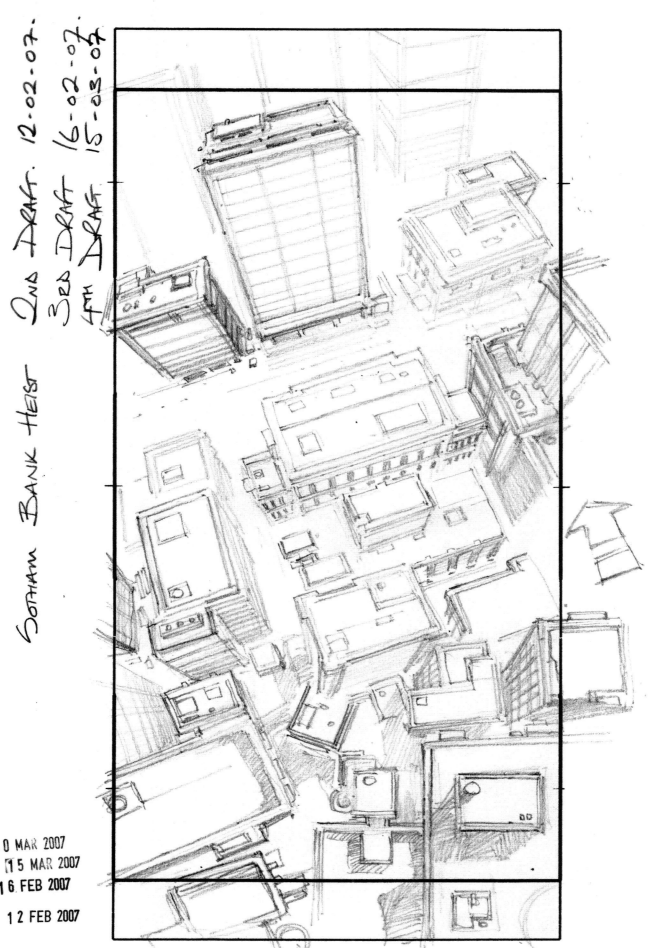

GOTHAM BANK HEIST

2nd DRAFT. 12·02·07.
3rd DRAFT. 16-02-07.
4th DRAFT. 15-03-07.

THE DARK KNIGHT

UNIVERSE
NEW YORK

THE DARK KNIGHT

FEATURING PRODUCTION ART AND FULL SHOOTING SCRIPT

Written by Craig Byrne

Designed by Mike Essl and Alexander Tochilovsky

Batman created by Bob Kane

UNIVERSE
NEW YORK

First published in the United States of America in 2008
by UNIVERSE PUBLISHING
A Division of Rizzoli International Publications, Inc.
300 Park Avenue South
New York, NY 10010
www.rizzoliusa.com

2008 2009 2010 2011 2012 / 10 9 8 7 6 5 4 3 2

Graphic Design: Mike Essl and Alexander Tochilovsky
DC Comics Editor: Steve Korté
Universe Editor: Jessica Fuller

Printed in the United States

ISBN-13: 978-0-7893-1812-1
Library of Congress Catalog Control Number: 2008902809

ACKNOWLEDGMENTS

Christopher Nolan, Emma Thomas, Charles Roven,
Jordan Goldberg, Nathan Crowley, Lindy Hemming,
Jonathan Nolan, David S. Goyer, Peter Robb-King,
Stephen Vaughn, John Caglione Jr, Lisa Perkins,
Dan Grace, Conor O'Sullivan, Jim Cornish, Stephen
Forrest Smith, Graham Churchyard, Jamie Rama,
Dan Walker, Peter Lando, Claudia Kalindjian, Phillis
Lehmer, Sarah Robinson, Ben Nowicki, Alex Klein,
Roy Button, Andy Horwitz, Joe Palmer, and Izzy Hyams.

A FILM BY CHRISTOPHER NOLAN

WARNER BROS. PICTURES PRESENTS

IN ASSOCIATION WITH LEGENDARY PICTURES A SYNCOPY PRODUCTION A FILM BY CHRISTOPHER NOLAN CHRISTIAN BALE "THE DARK KNIGHT" MICHAEL CAINE HEATH LEDGER GARY OLDMAN AARON ECKHART MAGGIE GYLLENHAAL AND MORGAN FREEMAN MUSIC BY HANS ZIMMER JAMES NEWTON HOWARD COSTUME DESIGNER LINDY HEMMING EDITOR LEE SMITH, A.C.E. PRODUCTION DESIGNER NATHAN CROWLEY DIRECTOR OF PHOTOGRAPHY WALLY PFISTER, A.S.C. EXECUTIVE PRODUCERS BENJAMIN MELNIKER MICHAEL E. USLAN KEVIN DE LA NOY THOMAS TULL BASED UPON BATMAN CHARACTERS CREATED BY BOB KANE AND PUBLISHED BY DC COMICS STORY BY CHRISTOPHER NOLAN & DAVID S. GOYER SCREENPLAY BY JONATHAN NOLAN AND CHRISTOPHER NOLAN PRODUCED BY CHARLES ROVEN EMMA THOMAS CHRISTOPHER NOLAN DIRECTED BY CHRISTOPHER NOLAN

   PG-13 PARENTS STRONGLY CAUTIONED
Some Material May Be Inappropriate for Children Under 13.
INTENSE SEQUENCES OF VIOLENCE AND SOME MENACE Soundtrack Album on Warner Sunset / Warner Bros. Records TM & © DC Comics WARNER BROS. PICTURES
©2008 Warner Bros. Ent. All Rights Reserved

WWW.THEDARKKNIGHT.COM

PAGES 2-3 Batman's "garage" (in reality a garage in the home of director Christopher Nolan and his wife, The Dark Knight producer Emma Thomas).

PAGES 4-5 The Joker waits patiently in the interrogation room of the Gotham City Major Crimes Unit.

PAGES 6-7 An assortment of Joker cards

THE DARK KNIGHT

Three years after the release of *Batman Begins*, Christopher Nolan's extremely successful reinvention of the Caped Crusader, the legendary hero has returned to Gotham City in *The Dark Knight*. The new film not only continues the story, but it also reinvents Batman's most famous villain, the Joker, in a plot hinted at during the conclusion of *Batman Begins*.

Creating a sequel gave the film's designers as well as director Nolan a chance to explore new aspects and designs for their lead character and the city he protects, in addition to taking Batman to new locales. Settings and plans were also developed for other icons of DC Comics lore such as Harvey Dent and the Falcone crime family.

One of the first priorities for costume designer Lindy Hemming was to redesign the Batman uniform for the second film. "The only thing I didn't get a chance to do for the first film was to redesign the Batsuit," Hemming explains. "Partly through my not having the confidence to change something which was so established, and partly because it was our first go at Batman, so we all felt we [had to] respect what had been done before, so our changes to the suit were quite minimal."

LEFT *Batman surges through the streets of Gotham City on the Bat-Pod, a sleek new vehicle created especially for The Dark Knight.*

"All of the previous films had one kind of suit, which was taking a whole outer body as though the man was putting on a body, but the logic of that seemed quite difficult to me," Hemming explains. "So we looked at all sorts of under-armor suits that they use for motor-biking, and what the Army uses underneath [their uniforms, such as] Kevlar plates that slip into things."

Increased comfort for actor Christian Bale also factored in the redesign. "There was the whole issue of the rubber of the previous suits, which made it so uncomfortable for the actor, sweating and not being able to sit down properly," Hemming says. "So we set about redesigning the suit as a much airier, much more modern, much more subtle piece of equipment, like a suit of armor instead of a rubber suit." Using different materials still would maintain the general look of the Batman outfit, however. "Of course, the most important thing all the time is to maintain the silhouette of everything, so that you do look at him in the dark, and you think, 'It's Batman'," Hemming says.

"Batman still needed protection, but Chris wanted to bring in this flexibility," says Batsuit costume supervisor Graham Churchyard. "We decided that smaller armored plates would allow a crumple zone between those armored plates, and allow Batman more movement. That's really how it developed."

"When you look at it closer, we see that [the suit] is made up of many more facets, and the pieces are moving more," Hemming reveals. "Then under that again, there's [a material] like a titanium steel mesh that prevents him from being damaged. I'm really pleased with it. I think it looks good."

A major concern for costume designer Hemming, director Nolan, and actor Christian Bale was the lack of neck movement in previous incarnations of the Batsuit—a problem that has now been solved for *The Dark Knight*. The solution was to simply divide the head cowl from the neck. In *The Dark Knight*, this change is made because Bruce Wayne tells Lucius Fox that he wants the suit to be lighter, faster, and more agile—although in fact, the weight of the suit did not change very much.

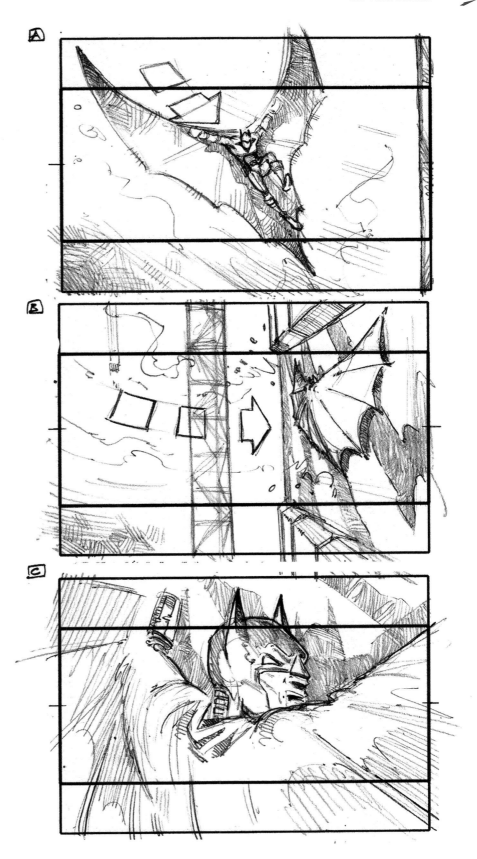

PAGE 10 *Production artwork by Lindy Hemming conceptualizing the mesh underarmor of the Batsuit*

PAGE 11 *Suited up and ready to protect— Christian Bale as Batman*

TOP LEFT *Batman approaches the unfinished Prewitt Building.*

BOTTOM LEFT *Batman watches over Gotham City.*

RIGHT *Storyboard art for a sequence that never made it into the film*

LEFT *Atop the rooftops of Hong Kong, Batman prepares to fire a sticky bomb that will soon blast open a building.*

TOP RIGHT *Designs for the sticky bomb gun, the newest weapon in Batman's arsenal*

BOTTOM RIGHT *Storyboard art showing the sticky bomb gun in action*

"The truth is that is isn't lighter," Hemming concedes. "But it is more agile, it's easier to wear, and Christian doesn't get so hot. Those are the real practical truths about it. All of the little panels and tiny pieces mount up, and it's made up of over 100 pieces, but hopefully all of those things, like being able to take the hard part of your head off and having only a lightweight mesh underneath, all make Christian's life much better."

"No one on Earth wants to wear a Batsuit," Hemming says with a laugh, "but if you have to, I think this one is better."

Batman's cape was another consideration when reworking the Batsuit. "The cape is the same as last time; we didn't want to redesign it. In fact, we spent a lot of time on the cape for *Batman Begins*, because we were trying to fulfill the comic convention that his cape looks different at different times. It's this huge, long billowing thing in emotional moments, but when he's fighting, of course, it's retracted and not quite so voluminous," Hemming explains. For the new film, and especially because of the introduction of the new Bat-Pod vehicle, some alternate ideas for cape retraction came into play. "I wanted to make a kind of backpack, where the whole cape could withdraw into the backpack," she reveals. "I sort of researched the shape of a bat's wings and worked out that it could flip repeatedly at 100 miles an hour, and end up as a kind of a backpack-shaped thing on Batman's back. Originally I think that was going to happen every time he got on the Bat-Pod, but in the end, Chris really wanted to have the flowing cape, so we opted for a shorter version of the cape for when Batman rides the Bat-Pod."

The last alteration to the Batsuit for the new film were be the gauntlets on Batman's arms. "Story-wise, the gauntlets have moved on a stage," costume supervisor Churchyard says. "Whereas, in *Batman Begins*, he'd taken these Tibetan gauntlets and sprayed them black as part of his costume, they have now become a sort of functional weapon, and the double scallops on these gauntlets actually fly out like throwing stars. They're very impressive."

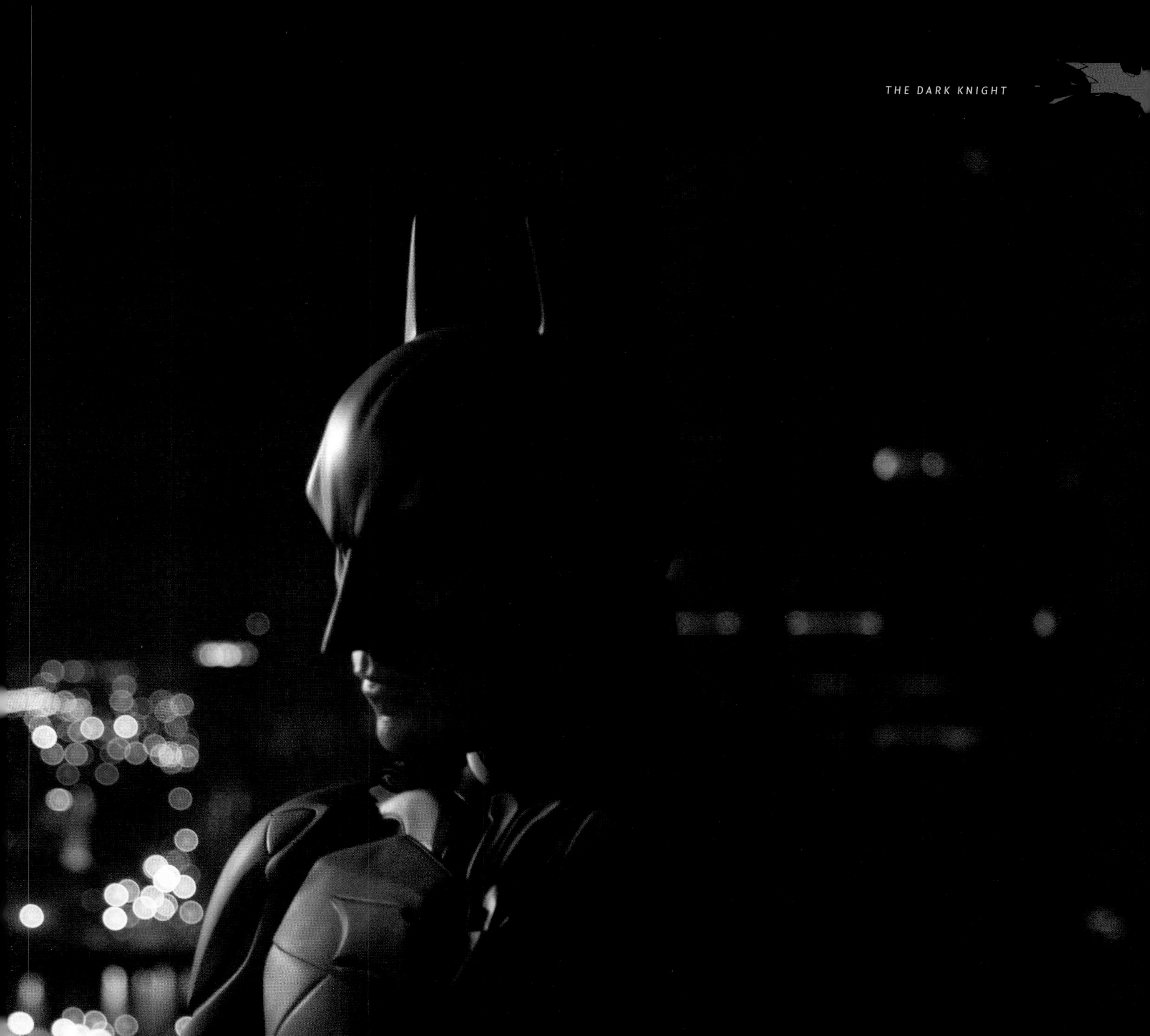

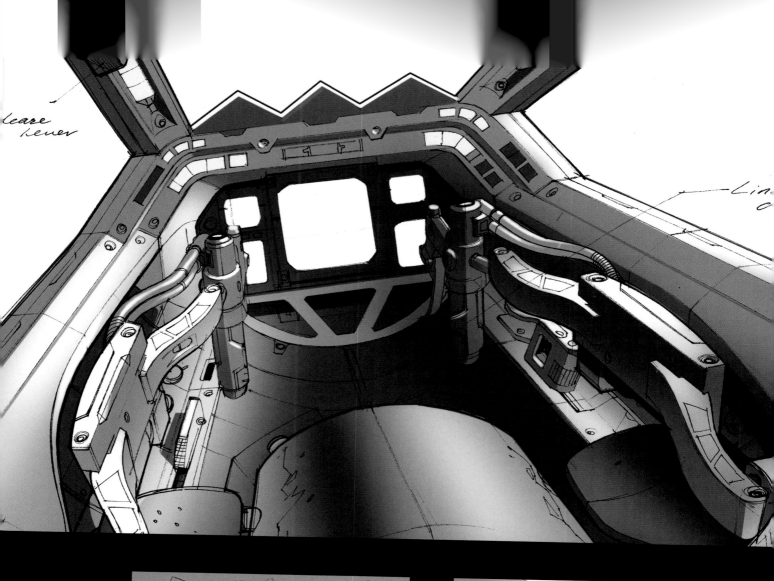

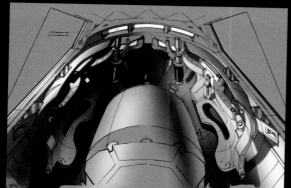

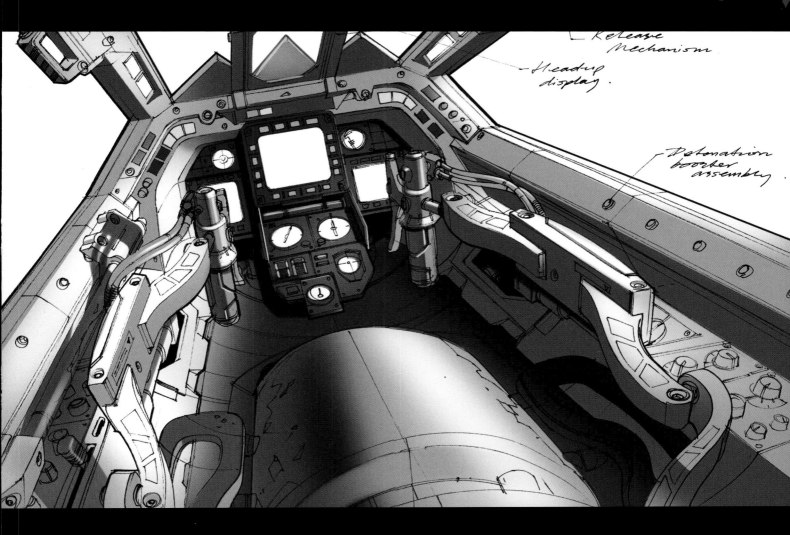

Release
Mechanism

Headup
display.

Detonation
booster
assembly

PAGES 16-17 *Light reflects off the new Batsuit, though it is still dark enough to allow Batman to disappear into shadows.*

ABOVE AND LEFT *Designs for the pod-interior of the Tumbler that will soon transform itself into Batman's newest vehicle: the Bat-Pod*

RIGHT *Storyboard: Batman prepares for the Bat-Pod to break away from the Batmobile.*

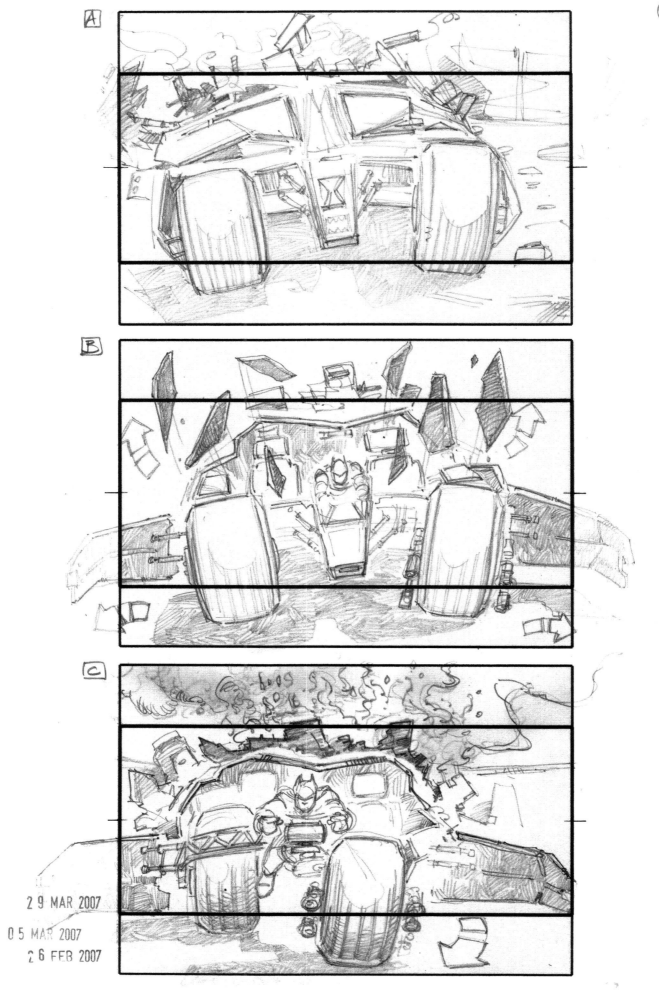

57.

A

B

C

2 9 MAR 2007

0 5 MAR 2007

2 6 FEB 2007

A

B

FEB 2007

C

2 9 MAR 2007

With *Batman Begins* we got to introduce the Batmobile and the Batsuit. But at the same time we didn't jump into the fully formed world of Batman with all of the gadgetry," Christopher Nolan says. "What we get to do in continuing the story is to show how that evolves and how that becomes more high-tech and more expanded, but still in a credible way, in a real-world timeline. What I love about Batman and tried to bring to both of these films is the sense that these things really are possible. He has no superpowers except for his extraordinary wealth."

The two-wheeled Bat-Pod was a new creation for both *The Dark Knight* and Batman's world, very different from anything presented before. "We've never quite seen anything like this on the street," production designer Nathan Crowley says with enthusiasm.

As fabulous as the Batmobile is, Batman needs a vehicle where he can have more manoeuvrability, get into tighter spaces that the Batmobile can't go," says producer Charles Roven. "So he develops the Bat-Pod, which is a motorcycle of sorts, but it has machine guns and rockets, and it can go almost anywhere.

In designing the Bat-Pod, the intention was to get away from the conventions of a traditional motorcycle. "It really had to belong to the same family as the Batmobile, and not just be a motorcycle or a machine," Crowley explains.

To create the vehicle, Crowley and his team went to Chris Nolan's garage and made models, trying to find the best shapes. "After about four or five models, we found the shape, and then we thought, 'You know what? Let's just build it full-size in this garage. Let's go for it'," Crowley recalls. The original Bat-Pod design was made out of plastic drainpipes and any materials that could be found. "It's one thing making a model of a car and sizing that up," Crowley says, "but although [that's] hard, it's not as hard as sizing up a motorbike and seeing if the proportions look correct. We decided to build it at full size, and then got special effects in to see if they could build it. Of course, they were horrified that they might have to actually mechanize this thing!"

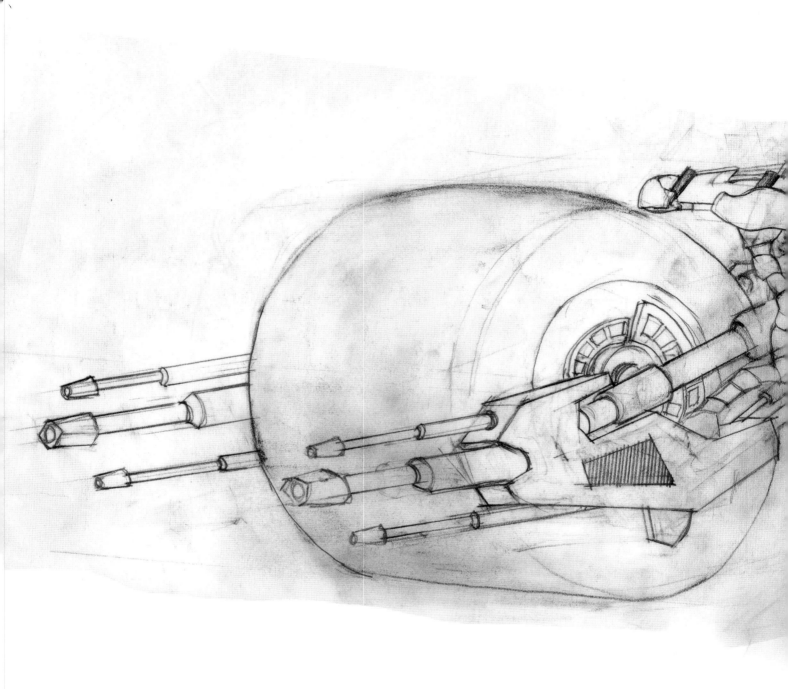

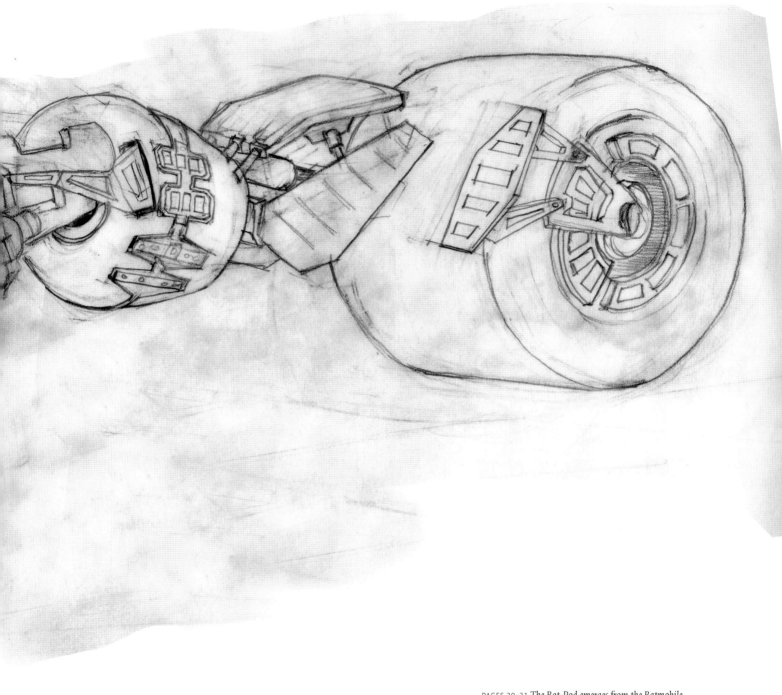

PAGES 20-21 *The Bat-Pod emerges from the Batmobile in this storyboard sequence.*

PAGES 22-21 *The versatile Bat-Pod can maneuver through anything, even a mall within the Gotham train station!*

ABOVE *An early Bat-Pod conceptual drawing*

Before building a full-size model of the Bat-Pod, production designer Nathan Crowley created miniatures and eventually, a full-size model. Note the evolution in color and design.

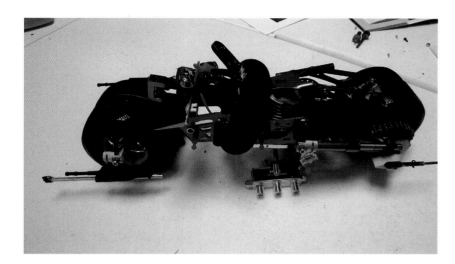

Crowley was aware that building a functional Bat-Pod would be a challenge. "The task was to build something that could go really fast, make sharp turns, as well as the usual outrageous parameters that we set for special effects that we, as designers, create to make their lives hard but exciting," he says with a smile, "and they did it very well."

Fortunately, the team assembled by special effects supervisor Chris Corbould succeeded in bringing the Bat-Pod to functional life. "The drive train for it was completely unusual," Crowley notes. "It was a whole process. There was the usual clash of engineering versus design, and we wanted to keep the look of it, otherwise there was no point in making it.

"I would say we ended up with the sort of 'Phat Boy' version of the design," Crowley says. "It's very close. It's the muscly brother of the original design, which was much more spindly but allowed no room for engineering," he says.

ABOVE Bat-Pod digital imagery

RIGHT An early Bat-Pod model

FAR RIGHT Storyboards for the Bat-Pod sequence
and weapons

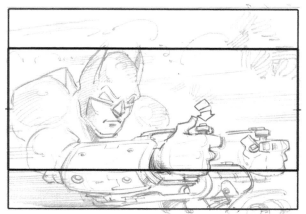

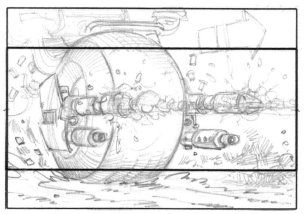

ABOVE AND FAR LEFT *Bruce Wayne's new Bat-Bunker houses surveillance monitors, banks of computers, the Batmobile, and the latest version of his Batsuit.*

LEFT *First introduced in Batman Begins, the Tumbler (AKA the Batmobile) can handle any terrain and can easily plow through anything in its path—including oncoming traffic.*

31

2 9 MAR 2007

Storyboards and realization of one of the film's most
exciting chase sequences

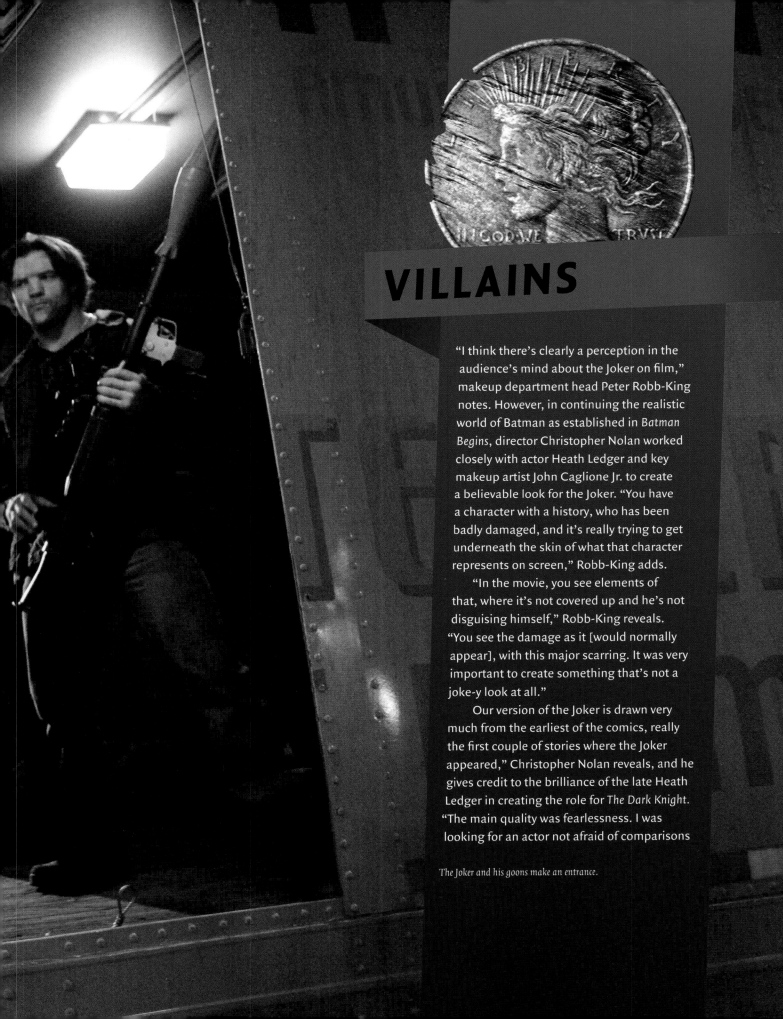

VILLAINS

"I think there's clearly a perception in the audience's mind about the Joker on film," makeup department head Peter Robb-King notes. However, in continuing the realistic world of Batman as established in *Batman Begins*, director Christopher Nolan worked closely with actor Heath Ledger and key makeup artist John Caglione Jr. to create a believable look for the Joker. "You have a character with a history, who has been badly damaged, and it's really trying to get underneath the skin of what that character represents on screen," Robb-King adds.

"In the movie, you see elements of that, where it's not covered up and he's not disguising himself," Robb-King reveals. "You see the damage as it [would normally appear], with this major scarring. It was very important to create something that's not a joke-y look at all."

Our version of the Joker is drawn very much from the earliest of the comics, really the first couple of stories where the Joker appeared," Christopher Nolan reveals, and he gives credit to the brilliance of the late Heath Ledger in creating the role for *The Dark Knight*. "The main quality was fearlessness. I was looking for an actor not afraid of comparisons

The Joker and his goons make an entrance.

with previous actors, not afraid of taking on such an iconic role, and someone with a really strong point of view on how they'd approach that. Heath had those qualities in spades."

Keeping with Christopher Nolan's wishes to make all aspects of Batman's world as realistic as possible, the make up team including Robb-King, John Caglione Jr., and Conor O'Sullivan did medical research to ensure that the Joker's scarring looked genuine. "We didn't base it on any specific sort of injury; it was an amalgamation of things, and it came together really well," he says.

Prosthetic makeup artist Conor O'Sullivan points out that it was important to ground the Joker in reality rather than in complete fantasy. "The scarring was [designed] to give him the appearance of a smile, or a leer, but also, it could be responsible for the character losing his mind, in a way," he says.

Applying the Joker makeup was a complicated but enjoyable process for Heath Ledger and makeup artist John Caglione Jr. "Heath would scrunch up his face in specific expressions, raising his forehead, and squinting his eyes, and I would paint on the white over his facial contortions," Caglione says. "This technique created textures and expressions that just painting the face one flat white would not. Then I used black makeup around Heath's eyes while he held them closed very tight, which created consistent facial textures. Then after the black was on, I sprayed water over his eyes, and Heath would squeeze his eyes and shake his head side to side, and all this black drippy and smudgy stuff would happen. Doing Heath's makeup was like a dance."

"There are so many things that the Joker does in this movie," Robb-King continues. "They're not all good things, and they're not all pleasant things, but it's all done with an element of his character's name. The Joker is very powerful because he has so many people under his control. People are absolutely scared of him."

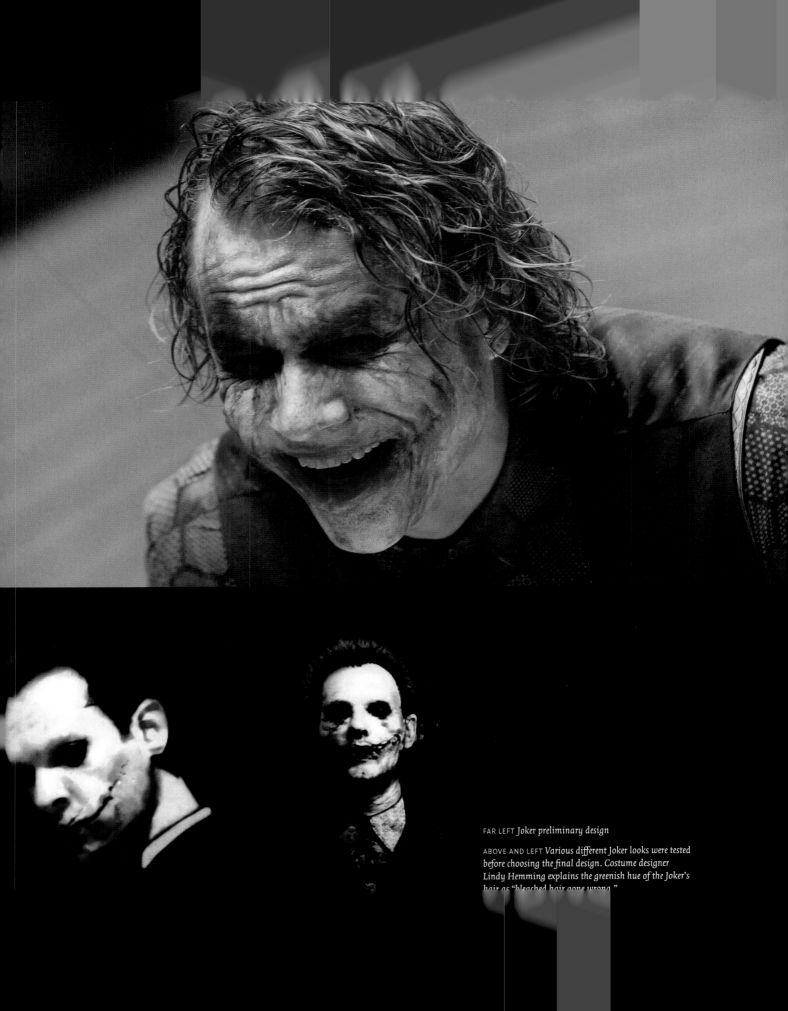

FAR LEFT *Joker preliminary design*

ABOVE AND LEFT *Various different Joker looks were tested before choosing the final design. Costume designer Lindy Hemming explains the greenish hue of the Joker's hair as "bleached hair gone wrong."*

JOKER....

JOKER — Heath Leger. "The Dark Knight."

Andy Henning Aug 2006. L.A.

A number of costume designs, ranging from traditional to the anarchic, were tested before settling on the Joker's final look.

For the Joker's costume, designer Lindy Hemming began creating her look with a lot of research, and every detail—including the shade of purple for his suit—was considered. Hemming also found art reference for clowns who had worn face paint that had sweated and dripped, creating a look that Hemming describes as "awful." When director Nolan gave her a picture of Francis Bacon's painting *Screaming Pope*, Hemming says that the look of the Joker started coming together.

Hemming also looked to the fashion designs of Vivienne Westwood for inspiration. "There was [a combination] of what people would wear now, which is modern, but there's also a retro, sort of foppish feeling to it," she says. "I knew for certain that in the Sex Pistols Johnny Rotten did do that. He always dressed in these amazing tailored suits, but they were in these horrible, vile colors."

In Milan, Hemming found a pair of shoes that would complete the Joker outfit. Although the shoes had a swoop up at the front, they were not clown shoes. "When Heath came along and we showed him all these bits, he really went for it," she reveals.

Despite previous popular looks for the Joker, the entire crew felt it was important for the Joker to have a new and different look for The Dark Knight. "I don't think we ever slavishly copy anything, because we're not really copyists," Peter Robb-King says. "That's the whole point with these films. We are creating characters that the audience can believe in, that could physically be real, and that is what's exciting."

"I'm not worried that it doesn't look like the comic-book Joker or from the previous Batman films," Conor O'Sullivan adds. "It's just different, and it has much more of a realism about it, which I think makes it a bit more disturbing. You can really appreciate why somebody would lose his mind if he had something like that happen to him, and reality is always more disturbing than fantasy."

"I think it was great to go down the angle of the sort of Clockwork Orange anarchist," Nathan Crowley enthuses. "To me, that was the perfect way to go."

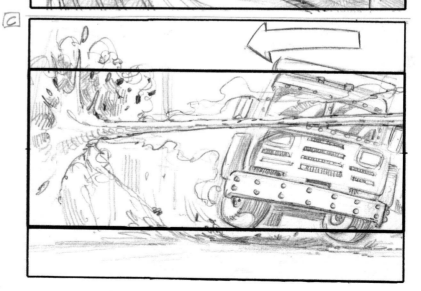

LEFT The Joker and his gang attack an armored car in this sequence.

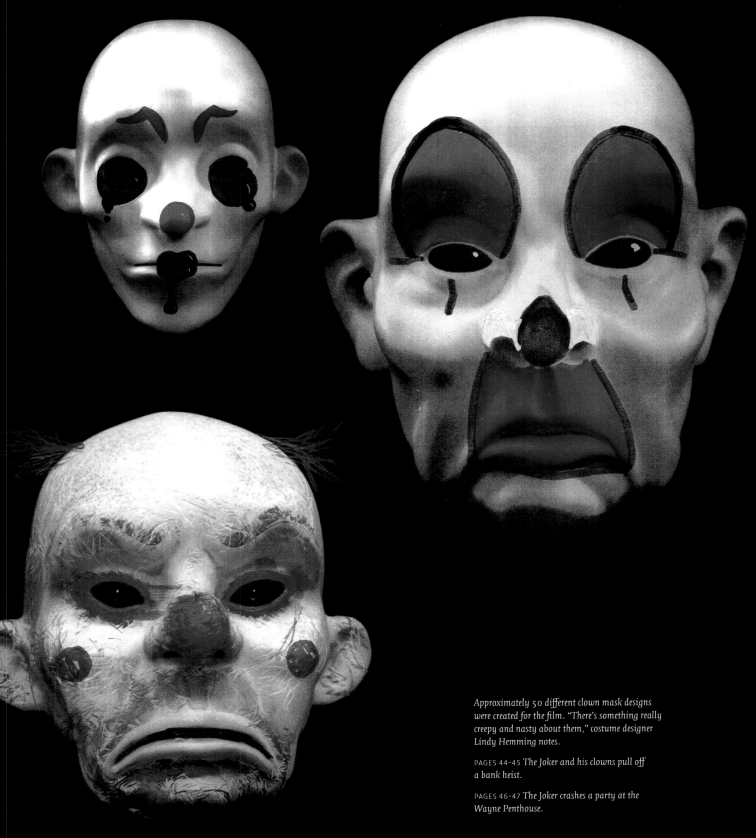

Approximately 50 different clown mask designs were created for the film. "There's something really creepy and nasty about them," costume designer Lindy Hemming notes.

PAGES 44-45 The Joker and his clowns pull off a bank heist.

PAGES 46-47 The Joker crashes a party at the Wayne Penthouse.

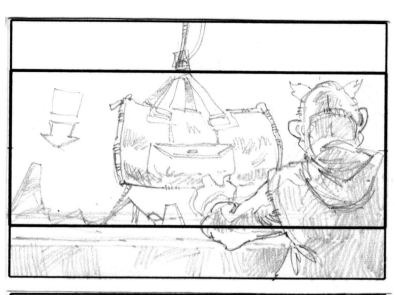

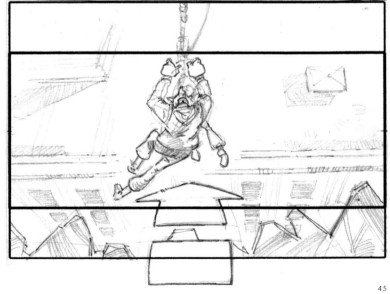

The Joker has finally pushed Batman to his limits.

The Joker gets his pile of cash, but he cares more about
mayhem than money.

A

Costumes, makeup and visual effects all played important roles in the creation of Two-Face, the other major villain introduced in *The Dark Knight*. "Other than the Joker, I think that Harvey Dent is the most interesting of the Batman characters left to deal with," Christopher Nolan says. "The real story of Harvey Dent, who he is and what he represents about Gotham and then what happens to him, is a very grand-scale story."

The gruesome visage of Two-Face was created first in concept sketches, next in clay sculptures, and finally through visual effects. Makeup department head Peter Robb-King says, "We worked closely with Nick Davis, who is visual effects supervisor, to create the severe damage that's done to [Harvey's] face, because the damage is so deep that we're going to see parts of the anatomy that you couldn't achieve prosthetically. It's such a deep chasm in parts of his face."

"The makeup process was interesting," says Aaron Eckhart, who portrays Harvey Dent and his deranged alter-ego, Two-Face. "Because of technology, I didn't have to spend three, four hours in makeup every day, and then two hours taking it off. What they did was CGI, computer generated images. So half my face was covered in dots, white dots and black dots. Somehow the cameras could figure that out, and then figure out the motion of my face."

ABOVE LEFT *Clay models show the horrible facial scarring that befalls district attorney Harvey Dent.*

FAR LEFT *Storyboard art showcases the two sides of Two-Face.*

LEFT *Harvey Dent's two-headed lucky coin, just like its owner, becomes horribly scarred.*

PAGES 56-57 *Two-Face's coin plays a role in a twisted game of Russian roulette.*

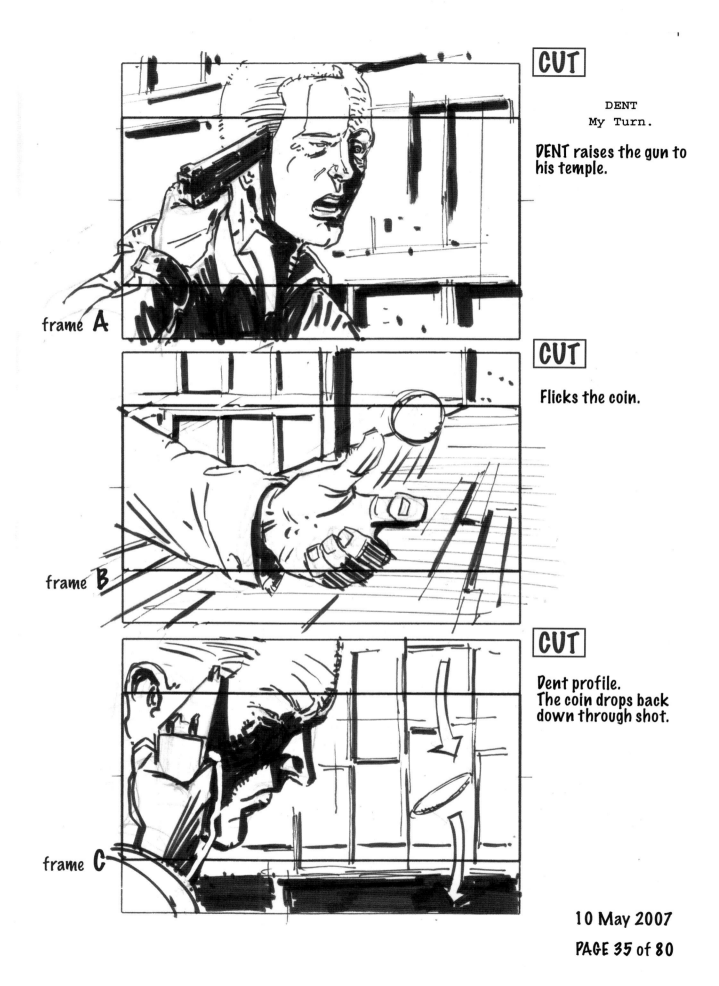

CUT

DENT
My Turn.

DENT raises the gun to his temple.

CUT

Flicks the coin.

CUT

Dent profile.
The coin drops back down through shot.

frame A

frame B

frame C

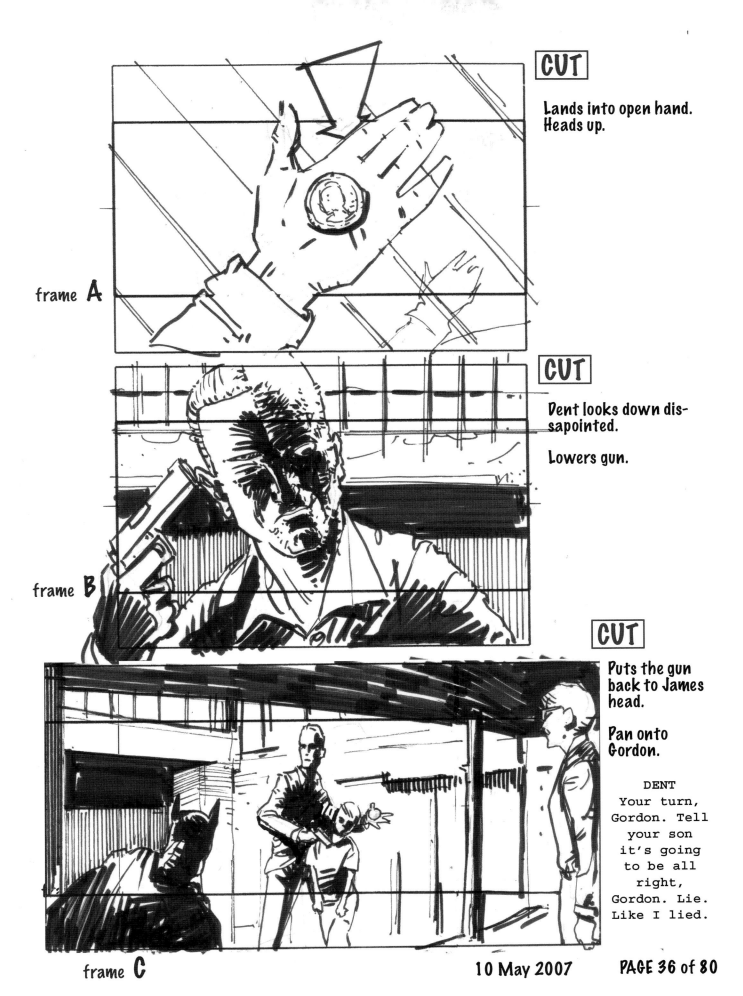

CUT

Lands into open hand.
Heads up.

frame A

CUT

Dent looks down dis-
sapointed.

Lowers gun.

frame B

CUT

Puts the gun
back to James
head.

Pan onto
Gordon.

DENT
Your turn,
Gordon. Tell
your son
it's going
to be all
right,
Gordon. Lie.
Like I lied.

frame C

10 May 2007   PAGE 36 of 80

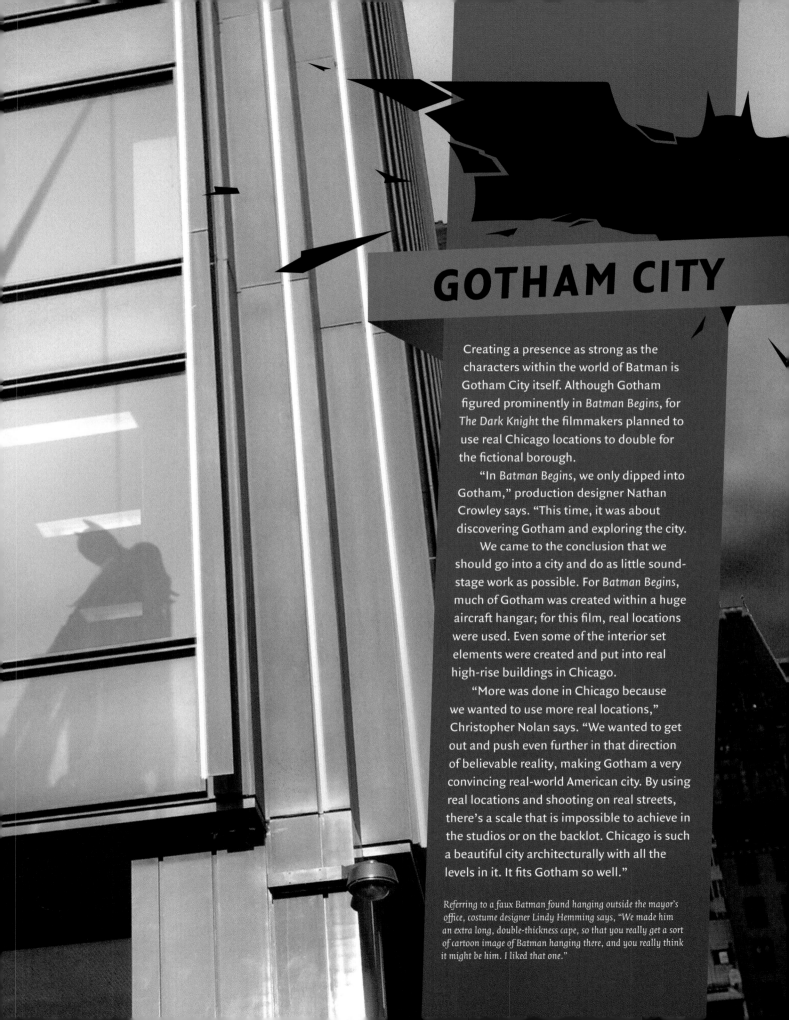

GOTHAM CITY

Creating a presence as strong as the characters within the world of Batman is Gotham City itself. Although Gotham figured prominently in *Batman Begins*, for *The Dark Knight* the filmmakers planned to use real Chicago locations to double for the fictional borough.

"In *Batman Begins*, we only dipped into Gotham," production designer Nathan Crowley says. "This time, it was about discovering Gotham and exploring the city. We came to the conclusion that we should go into a city and do as little sound-stage work as possible. For *Batman Begins*, much of Gotham was created within a huge aircraft hangar; for this film, real locations were used. Even some of the interior set elements were created and put into real high-rise buildings in Chicago.

"More was done in Chicago because we wanted to use more real locations," Christopher Nolan says. "We wanted to get out and push even further in that direction of believable reality, making Gotham a very convincing real-world American city. By using real locations and shooting on real streets, there's a scale that is impossible to achieve in the studios or on the backlot. Chicago is such a beautiful city architecturally with all the levels in it. It fits Gotham so well."

Referring to a faux Batman found hanging outside the mayor's office, costume designer Lindy Hemming says, "We made him an extra long, double-thickness cape, so that you really get a sort of cartoon image of Batman hanging there, and you really think it might be him. I liked that one."

"Obviously, with this type of film, you still have to deal with elements that you just can't create outside. There are certain stunt elements, and there are visual effects elements that require you to film inside, so we built sets inside real buildings, and that took many months to prepare," Crowley says.

"The views were real, though we did have to enhance those views, because Gotham is the biggest city in the United States," he explains. "But, the basis [of Chicago] gives us a natural rawness that being on a soundstage wouldn't give you. I think the fact that we got into some of these buildings, the fact we used real locations and we built into them, gave us a huge scale and a reality that is otherwise hard to achieve."

In decorating a set such as the mayor's office, set decorator Peter Lando tried to figure out the kind of person that would inhabit that space before adding the flourishes. "I often write a bio for each character. It makes my job a whole lot easier to think about where they've come from or where they're going; why they are where they are, and who they are."

"You have to situate these people in the story and give them a reason for being there and for what they're doing," Lando continues. "What I use decoration for is creating those possibilities, giving them a future, giving them a past, and making them belong in the story. As a set decorator, I don't choose the locations. I'm given locations, and I have to make the location work."

Another perspective of the imposter Batman, this time from within the mayor's office

"The mayor has an office in the corner, and his office is kind of glitzy, but there are no books in there. He's a lightweight," Lando explains. "You have to create a life for a person on a desktop. Sometimes that's the only tableau you have. It's the chair they choose to sit in. The kind of lamp they have. You're always looking at their social standing. Everything we choose is intensely personal."

"Because Wayne Manor burned down in *Batman Begins*, Bruce and Alfred have moved into the city. They're living in Bruce's penthouse. So the whole film has a completely different look; it has a much more urban, modern feeling, and the architecture of the movie is all clean lines," producer Emma Thomas says.

"We started realizing that we could come under the city, maybe have a secret passageway," Crowley recalls, "and Chicago allows you to do that, either by the underground roadways, or going through the rail tracks into the city, under the city. We came up with this bunker idea, that he's just hiding underground, and it's really just a concrete box. In some ways, it forms back into that modernist architectural element in that it's vast but it's very plain. It's just concrete.

"Another conclusion that we came up with is that it might not be secure enough, so everything has to be behind the concrete wall. Everything comes out of the ground or out of the walls and can be shut away. If you walk in there, you're essentially walking into what looks like an underground car park, but it is actually the Bat-Bunker," Crowley says. "It was a simplistic set that still had some vast visual interest. It was about proportion and perspective, which was great fun to do."

Inside the Wayne Enterprises research and development room, Bruce Wayne demonstrates his new voice-recognition software to a displeased Lucius Fox.

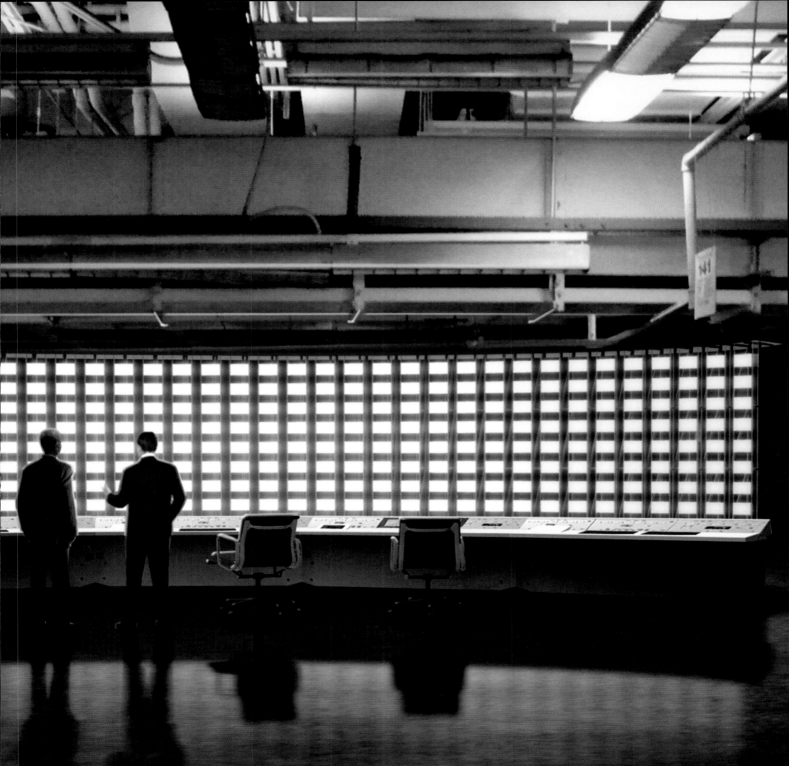

Visualizing the damage: The Joker's chaotic crime
spree hits a high point as the Gotham City hospital
and warehouses explode. Finding the right
buildings available for demolition in the Chicago
area was a challenge for the movie's location scouts.

THE DARK KNIGHT

by
Jonathan Nolan and Christopher Nolan

story by
Christopher Nolan & David S. Goyer

Batman created by
Bob Kane

T H E D A R K K N I G H T

BURNING. Massive flames. A dark shape emerges- The BAT
SYMBOL. Growing. Filling the screen with BLACKNESS.

                                                    CUT
                                                    TO:

DAYLIGHT. Moving over the towers of downtown Gotham...
Closing in on an office building... On a large window...
Which SHATTERS to reveal-

INT. OFFICE, HIGH RISE -- DAY

A man in a CLOWN MASK holding a SMOKING SILENCED PISTOL
ejects a shell casing. This is DOPEY. He turns to a
second man, HAPPY, also in clown mask, who steps forward
with a CABLE LAUNCHER, aims at a lower roof across the
street and FIRES a cable across. Dopey secures the line to
an I-beam line- CLAMP on- sends a KIT BAG out then steps
OUT the window...

EXT. HIGH-RISE -- DAY

...into space. The men SLIDE across the DIZZYING DROP...
landing on the lower roof across the street.

EXT. DOWNTOWN GOTHAM -- DAY

A MAN on the corner, back to us, holding a CLOWN MASK. An
SUV pulls up. The man gets in, puts on his mask. Inside
the car- two other men wearing CLOWN MASKS.

                    GRUMPY
            Three of a kind. Let's do this.

One of the Clowns looks up from loading his automatic
weapon.

                    CHUCKLES
            That's it? Three guys?

                    GRUMPY
            There's two on the roof. Every guy
            is an extra share. Five shares is
            plenty.

                    CHUCKLES

Six shares. Don't forget the guy
who planned the job.

                    GRUMPY
          Yeah? He thinks he can sit it out
          and still take a slice then I get
          why they call him the Joker.

Grumpy cocks his weapon. Bozo pulls the car over in front
of the GOTHAM FIRST NATIONAL BANK.

EXT. ROOFTOP, BANK -- CONTINUOUS

Dopey PRIES open an access panel-

                    HAPPY
          Why do they call him the Joker?

                    DOPEY
          I heard he wears make-up.

                    HAPPY
          Make-up?

Dopey pulls out thick bundles of blue CAT 5 cables.

                    DOPEY
          Yeah. To scare people. War paint.

EXT. BANK -- CONTINUOUS

Grumpy, Chuckles and Bozo get out of the car and march into
the bank CARRYING ASSAULT RIFLES-

INT. BANK -- DAY

The Security Guard looks up- Grumpy FIRES into the ceiling.
Customers SCREAM. Chuckles CRACKS the Security Guard.

As Grumpy and Bozo round up the hostages, one of the
TELLERS presses a button mounted beneath her window- a
SILENT ALARM.

EXT. ROOFTOP -- DAY

Dopey watches the alarm PING his handheld.

                    DOPEY
          Here comes the silent alarm.
               (touches a button)

                    And there it goes. That's funny.
                    It didn't dial out to 911- it was
                    trying to reach a private number.

Behind him, Happy RAISES his silenced HANDGUN.

                              HAPPY
                    Is it a problem?

                              DOPEY
                    No, no. I'm done here.

Happy SHOOTS. Dopey SLUMPS. Happy picks up his bag and
FORCES OPEN the roof access door...

INT. STAIRWELL, BANK -- DAY

...and speeds down the stairs, to the basement. He SLAMS
open the door...

INT. VAULT ROOM, BANK -- DAY

...and comes face to face with a huge VAULT.

INT. LOBBY, BANK -- DAY

Bozo and Grumpy move down the line of hostages- Bozo hands
each Hostage OBJECTS from a bag. A GRENADE. Grumpy
follows, PULLING THE PINS.

                              GRUMPY
                    Obviously, we don't want you doing
                    anything with your hands other than
                    holding on for dear life.

BLAM. Chuckles is BLOWN OFF HIS FEET- Grumpy and Bozo DIVE
for cover- the Bank Manager steps out of his office,
SHOTGUN in hand. Hostages SCRAMBLE, CLINGING their
grenades...

INT. VAULT ROOM, BANK -- DAY

Happy CLAMPS a DRILL to the vault- the bit SPINS- SLIDES
into the metal door- a BOLT of ELECTRICITY RIPS THROUGH THE
DRILL, THROWING HAPPY TO THE FLOOR-

INT. LOBBY, BANK -- DAY

Grumpy and Bozo cower as the Bank Manager FIRES again.

                    GRUMPY
              He's got three left?

Bozo raises TWO fingers. Grumpy squeezes off a SHOT. The
Bank Manager FIRES. FIRES again. Grumpy looks at Bozo,
who nods. Grumpy JUMPS UP.

The Bank Manager FIRES- Grumpy GRUNTS as buckshot CLIPS his
shoulder. FALLS. The Bank Manager moves in for the kill,
FUMBLING for new shells. Bozo STANDS- SHOOTS him.

Bozo picks up the shotgun. Grumpy checks his wound- it's
superficial. He struggles to his feet.

                    GRUMPY (CONT'D)
              Where'd you learn to count?!

Bozo's mask stares him down. Grumpy heads for the stairs
in the back. Bozo starts loading fresh shells into the
shotgun.

                    BANK MANAGER
              You have any idea who you're
              stealing from? You and your
              friends are *dead*.

Bozo looks down at him. Says nothing.

INT. VAULT ROOM, BANK -- DAY

Happy at the vault door, barefoot, turning the tumblers
with hands stuffed into his SNEAKERS. Grumpy walks in.

                    HAPPY
              They wired this thing up with 5,000
              volts. What kind of bank does
              that?

                    GRUMPY
              A mob bank. Guess the Joker's as
              crazy as they say.

Happy shrugs. Grips the WHEEL BOLT and SPINS it.

                    GRUMPY (CONT'D)
              Where's the alarm guy?

                    HAPPY

                    Boss told me when the guy was done
                    I should take him out. One less
                    share.

                              GRUMPY
                    Funny, he told me something
                    similar...

Happy FREEZES. The wheel SPINS to a STOP- the vault DOOR
CLUNKS OPEN- Happy GRABS for his weapon- SPINS to see
Grumpy SHOOT. Grumpy steps over Happy into the vault...

INT. VAULT, BANK -- DAY

...which is filled with an eight-foot MOUNTAIN OF CASH.

INT. LOBBY, BANK -- DAY

Grumpy walks into the lobby, straining under several
DUFFELS filled with cash. He DUMPS them. Looks at Bozo.
LAUGHS.

                              GRUMPY
                    C'mon, there's a lot to carry...

INT. LOBBY, BANK -- DAY

Bozo walks back into the lobby with two more DUFFELS. Sets
them down on an ENORMOUS PILE. Grumpy looks at it.

                              GRUMPY
                    If this guy was so smart he would
                    have had us bring a bigger car.

Grumpy JABS his pistol in Bozo's back. Takes his weapon.

                              GRUMPY (CONT'D)
                    I'm betting the Joker told you to
                    kill me soon as we loaded the cash.

                              BOZO
                         (shakes head)
                    No. I kill the bus driver.

                              GRUMPY
                    Bus driver? What bus-

Bozo steps backwards. SMASH. Hostages SCREAM as the TAIL
END OF A YELLOW SCHOOL BUS ROCKETS through the front of the
bank, SLAMMING Grumpy into the teller's window.

Bozo picks up Grumpy's weapon. Another clown OPENS the
rear door of the bus. Bozo SHOOTS him. Then loads the
bags onto the bus. The wounded Bank Manager watches him.
In the distance: SIRENS.

> BANK MANAGER
> Think you're smart, huh? Well, the
> guy who hired you's just do the
> same to you...

Bozo slowly shakes his head.

> BANK MANAGER (CONT'D)
> Sure he will. Criminals in this
> town used to believe in things...

Bozo turns back to the Bank Manager. Crouches over him.

> BANK MANAGER (CONT'D)
> Honor. Respect. What do you
> believe, huh? What do you bel-

Joker slides a GRENADE into the man's mouth. A PURPLE
THREAD is knotted around the pin.

> THE JOKER
> I believe that what doesn't kill
> you...

Bozo PULLS off his MASK. The Bank Manager GASPS. In the
reflections of the glass DEBRIS behind the Bank Manager we
see GLIMPSES of a SCARRED MOUTH and CLOWN MAKEUP. THE
JOKER.

> THE JOKER (CONT'D)
> ...simply makes you *stranger*.

The Bank Manager's eyes go wide. The Joker rises, strolls
towards the bus, the purple thread attached to the grenade
pin UNRAVELLING FROM THE PURPLE LINING of his jacket as he
walks. The Joker climbs into the bus, SHUTS the rear door,
TRAPPING THE PURPLE THREAD...

EXT. SCHOOL, GOTHAM -- DAY

Kids pour out, heading onto a long line of school buses.

INT. BANK -- CONTINUOUS

As the bus pulls out, the purple thread PULLS THE PIN-
hostages scream and scurry away from the Bank Manager, who
shakes with fear as, with a FIZZ, the grenade does not
explode, but SPEWS RED SMOKE.

EXT. BANK -- DAY

The School Bus pulls free of the Bank wall and pulls out
onto the street, SLIDING INTO THE LINE OF IDENTICAL BUSES
HEADING PAST THE BANK. The buses trundle past COP CARS
racing up the street... and we-

                                                    CUT TO:

EXT. MOVING OVER GOTHAM -- NIGHT

From the top of a brick building a SHAFT OF LIGHT comes on.

EXT. VARIOUS LOCATIONS -- CONTINUOUS

A PATROLMAN looks up at the BAT-SIGNAL. Smiles. A DEALER
standing beside a car spots the signal. Steps back.

                    DEALER
          No, man. I don't like it tonight.

                    BUYER
          What're you, superstitious? You
          got more chance of winning the
          powerball than running into *him*...

INT. MAJOR CRIMES UNIT, GOTHAM CENTRAL -- NIGHT

DETECTIVE RAMIREZ, female, rookie detective, 30's, makes
coffee, watching a news show on the television.

ON SCREEN: The host, MIKE ENGEL, lays into the MAYOR.

                    ENGEL
          Mr Mayor, you were elected on a
          campaign to clean up the city...
          when are you going to start?

                    MAYOR
          Well, Mike-

                    ENGEL
          Like this so-called Batman- a lot
          of people say he's doing some good,

73

ENGEL
that criminals are running
scared... but I say NO. What kind
of hero needs to wear a mask? You
don't let vigilantes run around
breaking the law... where does it
end? Yet, we hear rumors that
instead of trying to arrest him the
cops are using him to do their
dirty work.

MAYOR
I'm told our men in the Major
Crimes Unit are close to an arrest.

RAMIREZ
Hey, Wuertz- the Mayor says you're
closing in on the Batman.

WUERTZ looks up, listless. Crumples up a paper.

WUERTZ
The investigation is ongoing.

He throws the paper at the trash. It rebounds off a board
headed 'BATMAN: SUSPECTS.' Lined with pictures: Abraham
Lincoln. Elvis. The Abominable Snowman.

EXT. ROOFTOP, MAJOR CRIMES UNIT -- NIGHT

Ramirez comes out onto the roof. LIEUTENANT GORDON sits by
a SEARCHLIGHT. She hands Gordon a cup of coffee.

RAMIREZ
Ever intending to see your wife
again, Lieutenant?

GORDON
I thought you had to go look after
your mother, detective.

RAMIREZ
They checked her back into
hospital.

GORDON
I'm sorry.

RAMIREZ
(making light)

                    Least there she's got someone round
                    the clock. Unlike your wife.
                         (looks at bat-
                         signal)
                    He hasn't shown?

Gordon gets up. Looks into the sky at the bat-signal.

                         GORDON
                    Often doesn't. But I like
                    reminding everybody that he's out
                    there.

                         RAMIREZ
                    Why wouldn't he come?

                         GORDON
                    Hopefully... Because he's busy.

EXT. PARKING GARAGE -- NIGHT

Two black SUV's pull onto the top floor. A large man
emerges- the CHECHEN. A BODYGUARD points at the sky. The
Chechen peers up at the BAT-SIGNAL. Shrugs.

                         CHECHEN (IN RUSSIAN)
                    That's why we bring dogs.

BODYGUARD 2 opens the back door- three enormous ROTWEILERS
emerge, GROWLING. The Chechen crouches, KISSING the dogs.

                         CHECHEN (IN RUSSIAN) (CONT'D)
                    My little princes...
                         (to bodyguards)
                    The Batman's invisible to you
                    fools... but my little princes...
                    they can find human meat in
                    complete darkness.

The Chechen moves to the second SUV, reaches in and DRAGS
out a skinny, wild-eyed JUNKIE by his hair.

                         JUNKIE
                         (babbling)
                    No! No get 'em off me! Off me!

The Chechen drags the Junkie towards a battered white van.
The van's REAR DOORS OPEN... two armed THUGS emerge,
carrying BARRELS... a third hovers in the dark interior.

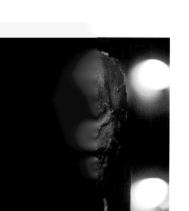

                    CHECHEN (ACCENTED ENGLISH)
          Look! Look what your drugs did to
          my customers!

                    VOICE (O.S.)
          Buyer beware...

The figure emerges: SCARECROW. Wearing his mask.

                    SCARECROW
          I told your man my compound would
          take you places. I never said
          they'd be places you *wanted* to go.

                    CHECHEN
          My business is *repeat* customers.

                    SCARECROW
          If you don't like what I have to
          offer, buy from someone else.

                    SCARECROW
          Assuming Batman left anyone else to
          buy from.

The Chechen frowns. THE DOGS START BARKING.

                    BODYGUARD
               (nervous)
          He's here.

A BURLY THUG at the periphery is suddenly SUCKED into the
darkness. In his place a shadow straightens, revealing
POINTED BAT-EARS against the glittering skyline.

                    CHECHEN
          Come on, sonofbitch- my dogs are
          hungry, pity there's only one of
          you...

A BODYGUARD to the side DISAPPEARS with a scream, and a
SECOND BAT-SHADOW appears.

The Chechen looks taken aback. Three more BAT-SHADOWS
appear... even the dogs stop growling.

BOOM! A hole appears in the SUV next to the Chechen. The
first bat-shadow steps into the light carrying a SHOTGUN.

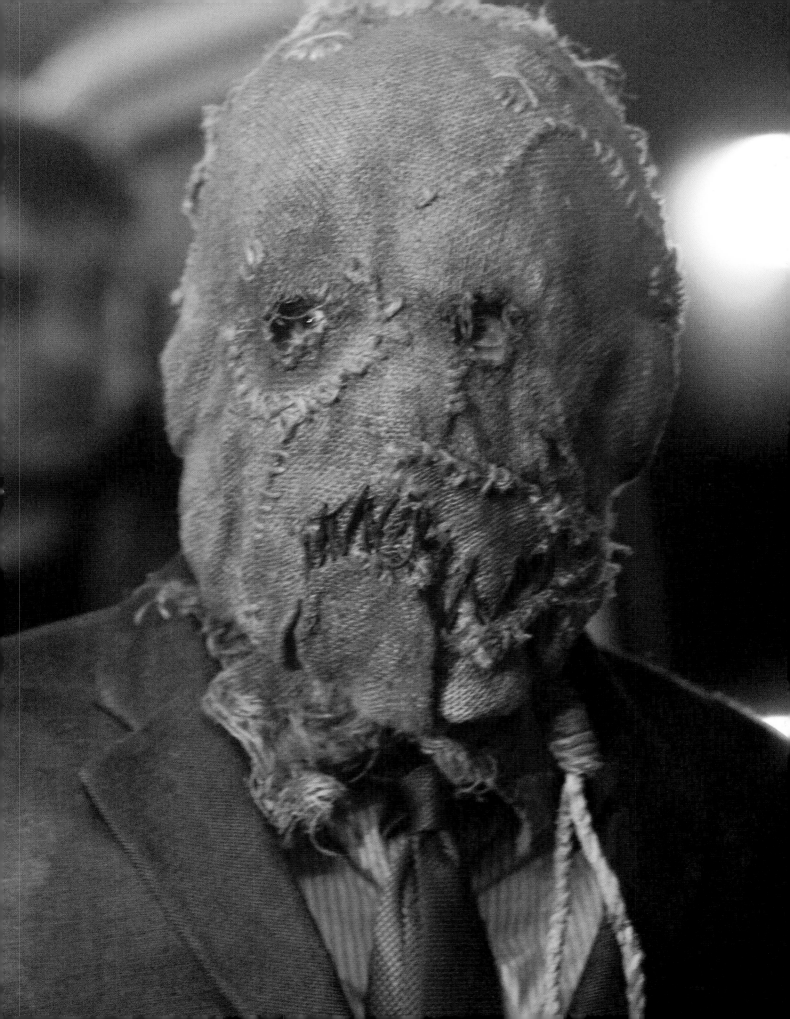

CHAOS as men scatter and the rooftop erupts in GUNFIRE.
The Chechen TURNS as he hears one of his men SCREAM.

> CHECHEN (CONT'D)
> Loose the dogs!

A Bodyguard releases the DOGS- they RACE, SALIVATING, into
the darkness...

The Dogs RACE towards a Bat-Shadow- the first dog LEAPS,
gets its JAWS around the Bat-Shadow's throat...

Scarecrow ducks behind the van- holes PUNCHED in the side
by shotgun blasts right behind him. He starts to climb
into the driver's seat-

The muzzle of a shotgun is pressed to the back of his head-
a bat-shadow is behind him- he SPRAYS him with FEAR TOXIN-
the bat-shadow collapses to the ground, SCREAMING. The
Cechnyan, cowering from gunfire, looks down at him.

> SCARECROW
> Not the real thing.

> CHECHEN
> How you know?

> SCARECROW
> We're old friends.

A HUGE BLACK SHAPE SLAMS down onto a row of parked cars.
The BATMOBILE.

> SCARECROW (CONT'D)
> That's more like it.

The Chechen's men BLAST away at the front of the car: the
bullets SPARK off its monstrous surface harmlessly...

INT. BATMOBILE -- CONTINUOUS

The cockpit is EMPTY. One of the screens reads "LOITER".
The shooting STOPS. The screen switches to "INTIMIDATE"

EXT. PARKING GARAGE -- CONTINUOUS

The men STARE at the Batmobile for a quiet moment... BOOM!
The Batmobile CANNONS blast cars all around the men-

A bat-shadow lines up his shotgun on a running bodyguard-
CLUNK- a BLACK GAUNTLET grasps the barrel and BENDS it
upwards with a HOWL of tortured steel- the bat-shadow looks
into the face of the Batman. The REAL BATMAN.

The Bat-shadow STUMBLES BACKWARDS in terror, leaving the
bent shotgun in Batman's hand. Batman OPENS his hand,
revealing a PNEUMATIC MANGLE hidden in his palm-

Batman bears down on the dogs mauling another bat-shadow-
DRAWS his GRAPPLING GUN and SHOOTS his grapple into the
fake Batman's leg and RIPS him from the dogs, one dog
HANGING ON as Batman pulls the unconscious man away... the
Chechen RUNS down the ramp towards the exit...

As Batman KICKS the dog off the fake Batman- the Chechen
gets into his SUV- another dog LOCKS ITS JAWS around
Batman's forearm, RIPPING, TEARING- Batman SWINGS THE DOG
OVER HIS HEAD- SMASHES it against the ground- its jaws
OPEN...

Batman rises, an engine RACES behind him- he can't turn in
time- BLAM- he's SLAMMED sideways by the speeding van.

INT. VAN -- CONTINUOUS

Scarecrow, driving, NODS at him and hits the gas... Batman
raises his hand, revealing his jointed mangle and pistons.
The mangle STRAIGHTENS and ROTATES from his palm to the
knife edge of his opened hand...

Batman CHOPS straight through the windshield- pulls his
hand out and CHOPS again- the mangle gets STUCK- Scarecrow
steers towards a column...

EXT. PARKING GARAGE -- CONTINUOUS

Batman can't free himself- he turns a dial on his forearm
piston- EXPLOSIVE BOLTS blow, freeing his gauntlet from the

mangle- he ROLLS free of the van as it SCRAPES the column
and barrels down the circular exit ramp.

Batman rises. A phony batman lying on the ground watches
as Batman climbs up to the edge of the ten-story corkscrew
ramp and stands there, waiting for something.

After a moment he JUMPS... and falls... ten stories...

He's about to hit the exit ramp- the van appears- his cape POPS OPEN- he SLAMS into the roof, CRUSHING the cab.

EXT. ROOFTOP, PARKING GARAGE -- MOMENTS LATER

The Chechen's men are lined up against the wall, bound with zip-ties. So are the fake batmen. Batman DUMPS Scarecrow next to the three "Batmen", RIPS his mask off.

> "BATMAN"
> We're trying to help you!

> BATMAN
> I don't need help.

> SCARECROW (O.S.)
> Not my diagnosis.

Batman silences Scarecrow with his boot. Turns to "Batman"

> BATMAN
> Don't let me find you out here
> again.

Batman moves towards the Batmobile.

> "BATMAN"
> You need us! There's only one of
> you- it's *war* out here!

Batman gets into the Batmobile.

> "BATMAN" (CONT'D)
> What gives *you* the right?! What's
> the difference between you and me?!

As the Canopy hisses shut-

> BATMAN
> I'm not wearing hockey pads.

The "Batman" looks down at his makeshift costume as the Batmobile ROARS past.

EXT. BANK -- NIGHT

LIEUTENANT GORDON ducks the barrage of SHOUTED QUESTIONS from press and picks his way into the lobby of the bank.

INT. LOBBY, BANK -- NIGHT

FORENSIC SPECIALISTS work the room. Ramirez hands Gordon
PRINTS- indicates the surveillance cameras.

                    RAMIREZ
          He can't resist showing us his
          face.

Gordon looks at the grainy blow-up of THE JOKER'S FACE:
sweating clown makeup plastered thick around the mouth.

                    GORDON
          Put this out, by morning we can put
          a big top over central holding and
          sell tickets. What's he hiding
          under that makeup?

Gordon approaches a FORENSIC PHOTOGRAPHER shooting Grumpy's
body. Gordon crouches to look at his clown mask. Batman
steps from the shadows. Gordon nods at Ramirez.

                    RAMIREZ
          Give us a minute, please, people!

The Forensic team and Ramirez leave. Gordon hands Batman
the blow-up of the Joker.

                    BATMAN
          Him again. Who are the others?

                    GORDON
          Another bunch of small timers.

Batman pulls a DEVICE from his belt- moves to the bundles
of cash scattered near the clown's body. The device PINGS.
Batman picks up a BUNDLE. Hands it to Gordon.

                    BATMAN
          Some of the marked bills I gave
          you.

                    GORDON
          My detectives have been making drug
          buys with them for weeks. This
          bank was another drop for the mob.
          That makes five banks- we've found
          the bulk of their dirty cash.

                    BATMAN
          Time to move in.

Gordon waves the photo.

                    GORDON
          What about this Joker guy?

                    BATMAN
          One man or the entire mob? He can
          wait.

                    GORDON
          We'll have to hit all banks
          simultaneously. SWAT teams,
          backup.

Gordon holds up the bundle of banknotes.

                    GORDON (CONT'D)
          When the new DA gets wind of this,
          he'll want in.

                    BATMAN
          Do you trust him?

                    GORDON
          Be hard to keep him out.

Gordon bags the cash.

                    GORDON (CONT'D)
          I hear he's as stubborn as you.

But Batman is already gone.

INT. WAYNE PENTHOUSE -- MORNING

Alfred walks past soaring downtown views as he carries a
breakfast tray through the vast, empty penthouse. He
stops, looking at a still-made bed. Alfred sighs, turns.

EXT. RAIL YARDS -- MORNING

Alfred gets out of the Rolls carrying a thermos. He walks
towards a RAILWAY BRIDGE, stops at a FREIGHT CONTAINER
sitting, lopsided, on blocks. Alfred unlocks the RUSTY
PADLOCK AND CHAIN. Steps inside.

INT. FREIGHT CONTAINER -- CONTINUOUS

Alfred FUMBLES in the dark- bangs his elbow- A HISS as the
FLOOR LOWERS... Alfred sinks down into...

INT. BAT-BUNKER -- CONTINUOUS

The container floor lowers on a giant PISTON. Alfred steps
off into a large, LOW-CEILINGED CONCRETE CHAMBER. The
Batmobile sits in the middle. Machines- 3d printers, power
tools- dot the high-tech space. At one end, Wayne sits at
a bank of monitors watching CCTV footage of the bank
robbery.

              ALFRED
      Be nice when Wayne Manor's rebuilt
      and you can swap not sleeping in a
      penthouse for not sleeping in a
      mansion.

Alfred places a cup of coffee in front of Wayne, who is
STITCHING up a cut on his arm.

              ALFRED (CONT'D)
        (takes needle)
      When you stitch yourself up you
      make a bloody mess.

              WAYNE
      But I learn about my mistakes.

              ALFRED
      You ought to be pretty
      knowledgeable by now, then.

              WAYNE
      My armor... I'm carrying too much
      weight- I need to be faster.

              ALFRED
      I'm sure Mr.Fox can oblige.
        (looks at wound)
      Did you get mauled by a tiger?

              WAYNE
      A dog.
        (off look)
      A *big* dog. There were more
      copycats last night, Alfred. With
      guns.

              ALFRED
      Perhaps you could hire some of them
      and take weekends off.

                    WAYNE
          This wasn't exactly what I had in
          mind when I said I wanted to
          inspire people.

                    ALFRED
          I know. But things *are* improving.
          Look at the new District
          Attorney...

Wayne indicates a monitor: a handsome MAN in a suit.

                    WAYNE
          I am. Closely. I need to know if
          he can be trusted.

Alfred looks at other images- the D.A. at a meeting.
Campaigning. Helping someone out of a cab: RACHEL.

                    ALFRED
          Are you interested in his
          character... or his social circle?

                    WAYNE
          Who Rachel spends her time with is
          her business.

                    ALFRED
          Well, I trust you're not following
          me on my day off.

                    WAYNE
          If you ever took one, I might.

Alfred bites the thread. Examines his stitches. Looks at
the SCARS criss-crossing Wayne's shoulders.

                    ALFRED
          Know your limits, Master Wayne.

                    WAYNE
          Batman has no limits.

                    ALFRED
          Well, *you* do, sir.

                    WAYNE
          I can't afford to know them.

                    ALFRED

And what happens the day you find
out?

               WAYNE
We all know how much you like to
say 'I told you so'.

               ALFRED
That day, Master Wayne, even I
won't want to. Probably.

INT. COURTROOM, SUPERIOR COURT -- DAY

HARVEY DENT bursts into the courtroom. Assistant D.A.
RACHEL DAWES, look up, ANNOYED.

               DENT
Sorry I'm late, folks.

Rachel leans in to Dent, speaking under her breath.

               RACHEL
Where were you?

               DENT
Worried you'd have to step up?

               RACHEL
I know the briefs backwards.

Dent pulls a large silver dollar out of his pocket. Grins.

               DENT
Well, then, fair's fair: heads,
I'll take it. Tails, he's all
yours.

Dent FLIPS. Shows it to Rachel- heads.

               RACHEL
You're flipping coins to see who
leads?

               DENT
My father's lucky coin. As I
recall, it got me my first date
with you.

               RACHEL

I'm serious, Harvey, you don't
leave things like this to chance.

                    DENT
          I don't.
              (sincere)
          I make my own luck.

Dent looks across at the defendant- SAL MARONI.

                    MARONI
          I thought the DA just played golf
          with the Mayor, things like that.

                    DENT
          Tee-off's 1:30. More than enough
          time to put you away for life,
          Sally.

The BAILIFFS lead a THIN MAN into the witness box. ROSSI.

INT. COURTROOM, SUPERIOR COURT -- DAY

Rossi takes a SIP of water. Dent works the room.

                    DENT
          With Carmine Falcone in Arkham,
          someone must've stepped up to run
          the so-called family.
              (Rossi nods)
          Is this man in the courtroom today?
              (Rossi nods again)
          Could you identify him for us,
          please?

Dent turns to Maroni, who is poker-faced. Dent smiles.

                    ROSSI
          You win, counselor. It was *me*.

Dent's smile disappears. He turns back to Rossi.

                    DENT
          I've got a sworn statement from you
          that *this* man, Salvatore Maroni, is
          the new head of the Falcone crime
          family.

                    ROSSI

                    Maroni? He's a fall guy. I'm the
                    brains of the organization.

LAUGHS from the gallery. Dent turns to the JUDGE.

                              DENT
                    Permission to treat the witness as
                    hostile?

                              ROSSI
                    Hostile? I'll show you *hostile*.

Rossi JUMPS UP, points a GUN at Dent's face. SCREAMS from
the gallery. Rossi PULLS the TRIGGER- the gun MISFIRES
with a POP. Dent steps forward, grabs the GUN- DECKS Rossi
with a RIGHT CROSS- unloads the GUN and sets it down in
front of Maroni.

                              DENT
                    Ceramic 28 caliber. Made in China.
                    If you want to kill a public
                    servant, Mr. Maroni, I recommend
                    you buy *American*.

Everyone STARES, open-mouthed, as Dent adjusts his tie.
The Bailiffs are wrestling Rossi from the box-

                              DENT (CONT'D)
                    But, your honor, I'm not done...

INT. LOBBY, DENT'S OFFICE, DA'S -- DAY

Rachel, excited, leads Dent through the lobby.

                              RACHEL
                    We'll never link the gun to Maroni,
                    so we can't charge him, but I'll
                    tell you one thing- the fact they
                    tried to kill you means we're
                    getting to them.

                              DENT
                    Glad you're so pleased, Rachel.
                    I'm fine by the way.

Rachel turns to Dent. Smooths his lapels.

                              RACHEL

Harvey, you're Gotham's D.A.- if
you're not getting shot at, you're
not doing your job.
(smiles)
'Course if you said you were
rattled we could take the rest of
the day...

                    DENT
          Can't. I dragged the head of the
          Major Crimes Unit down here.

                    RACHEL
          Jim Gordon? He's a friend- *try* to
          be nice.

INT. DENT'S OFFICE -- DAY

Gordon stands as Dent enters.   The two men shake.

                    GORDON
          Word is you've got a hell of a
          right cross. Shame Sal's going to
          walk.

                    DENT
          Well, good thing about the mob is
          they keep giving you second
          chances.

Dent picks up a bundle of bills from the heist.

                    DENT (CONT'D)
          Lightly irradiated bills. Fancy
          stuff for a city cop. Have help?

                    GORDON
          We liaise with various agencies-

                    DENT
          Save it, Gordon. I want to meet
          him.

                    GORDON
          Official policy is to arrest the
          vigilante known as Batman on sight.

                    DENT
          And that flood light on top of
          M.C.U.?

                    GORDON
          If you have any concerns about...
          malfunctioning equipment... take
          them up with maintenance,
          counselor.

Dent tosses the bills back onto his desk.   Annoyed.

                    DENT
          I've put every known money
          launderer in Gotham behind bars.
          But the mob is still getting its
          money out.   I think you and your
          "friend" have found the last game
          in town and you're trying to hit
          'em where it hurts: their wallets.
          Bold.   You gonna count me in?

                    GORDON
          In this town, the fewer people know
          something, the safer the operation.

                    DENT
          Gordon, I don't like that you've
          got your own *special* unit, and I
          don't like that it's full of cops I
          investigated at internal affairs.

                    GORDON
          If I didn't work with cops you'd
          investigated while you were making
          your name at I.A.- I'd be working
          alone.   I don't get political
          points for being an idealist- I
          have to do the best I can with what
          I have.

Dent looks at Gordon.   Considering how to proceed.

                    DENT
          You want me to back warrants for
          search and seizure on five banks
          without telling me who we're after?

                    GORDON
          I can give you the names of the
          banks.

                    DENT

> Well, that's a start. I'll get you
> your warrants. But I want your
> trust.

                    GORDON
             (rises)
> You don't have to sell me, Dent.
> We all know you're Gotham's white
> knight.

                    DENT
             (grins)
> I hear they've got a different
> nickname for me down at M.C.U..

Gordon smiles.

INT. BOARDROOM, WAYNE ENTERPRISES -- DAY

LUCIUS FOX, CEO of Wayne Enterprises, and the board listen
to LAU, 40s, CEO of L.S.I. Holdings.

                    LAU
> In China L.S.I. Holdings stands for
> dynamic new growth. A joint
> Chinese venture with Wayne
> Enterprises will be a powerhouse.

                    FOX
> Well, Mr.Lau, I speak for the rest
> of the board, and Mr.Wayne, in
> expressing our own excitement...

The Chinese look to the head of the table: Wayne, ASLEEP.

INT. HALLWAY, WAYNE ENTERPRISES -- DAY

Fox shows Lau to the elevator. He's joined by, REESE, 30s,
an ambitious M and A consultant lawyer.

                    LAU
> It's OK, Mr.Fox. Everyone knows
> who really runs Wayne Enterprises.

                    FOX
> We'll be in touch as soon as our
> people have wrapped up the
> diligence.

The elevator doors close. Reese frowns.

REESE
Sir, I know Mr.Wayne's curious how
his trust fund gets replenished but
frankly... it's embarrassing.

Fox heads for his office, Reese in tow.

FOX
You worry about the diligence, Mr.
Reese. I'll worry about Bruce
Wayne.

REESE
It's done- the numbers are solid.

FOX
     (smiles)
Do it again. Wouldn't want the
trust fund to run out, would we?

INT. BOARDROOM, WAYNE ENTERPRISES -- CONTINUOUS

Wayne is standing by the window.

FOX (O.S.)
Another long night?
     (Wayne smiles)
This joint venture was your idea,
and the consultants love it, but
I'm not convinced. L.S.I.'s grown
8 percent annually, like clockwork.
They must have a revenue stream
that's off the books. Maybe even
illegal.

WAYNE
OK. Cancel the deal.

FOX
     (looks at Wayne)
You already knew.

WAYNE
I needed a closer look at their
books.

Fox looks at Wayne. Wry.

FOX

Anything else you can trouble me
for?

                WAYNE
        I need a new suit.

                FOX
            (looks him over)
        Three buttons *is* a little nineties.

                WAYNE
        I'm not talking about fashion,
        Mr.Fox, so much as *function*.

Wayne pulls some diagrams. Fox looks them over.

                FOX
        You want to be able to turn your
        head?

                WAYNE
        Sure make backing out of the
        driveway easier.

                FOX
        I'll see what I can do.

INT. RESTAURANT -- NIGHT

Rachel and Dent at a table. Dent looks a little
intimidated by the surroundings.

                DENT
        It took three weeks to get a
        reservation *and* I had to tell them
        I worked for the government.

                RACHEL
        Really?

                DENT
        This city health inspector's not
        afraid to pull strings.

Rachel smiles. Then, over Dent's shoulder, she sees Wayne
enter, accompanied by a beautiful woman.

                DENT (CONT'D)
        What?

                    WAYNE
          Rachel! Fancy that.

                    RACHEL
          Yes, Bruce. Fancy that.

                    WAYNE
          Rachel, Natascha. Natascha,
          Rachel.

                    NATASCHA
               (Russian accent)
          Hello.

                    DENT
          The famous Bruce Wayne. Rachel's
          told me everything about you.

                    WAYNE
          I certainly hope not.

                    RACHEL
          Bruce, this is Harvey Dent.

                    WAYNE
          Let's put a couple tables together.

                    DENT
          I don't know if they'll let us-

                    WAYNE
          They should! I own the place.

                    RACHEL
          For how long? About three weeks?

                    WAYNE
          How'd you know?

                    RACHEL
          Natascha, aren't you...?

                    WAYNE
          Prima ballerina for the Moscow
          Ballet.

                    RACHEL
          Harvey's taking me next week.

                    WAYNE

You're into ballet, Harvey?

                    RACHEL
          No. He knows *I* am.

An extra table arrives.

INT. SAME -- LATER

They finish up dinner.

                    NATASCHA
          No, come on- *how* could you want to
          raise children in a city like this?

                    WAYNE
          I was raised here. I turned out
          OK.

                    DENT
          Is Wayne Manor *in* the city limits?

Rachel gives Dent a withering look.

                    WAYNE
          The Palisades? Sure. You know, as
          our new D.A. you *might* want to
          figure out where your jurisdiction
          ends.

                    NATASCHA
          I'm talking about the kind of city
          that idolizes a masked vigilante...

                    DENT
          Gotham's proud of an ordinary man
          standing up for what's right.

                    NATASCHA
          Gotham needs heroes like *you*-
          elected officials, not a man who
          thinks he's *above* the law.

                    WAYNE
          Exactly. Who appointed the Batman?

                    DENT
          We did. All of us who stood by and
          let scum take control of our city.

Wayne watches Dent.   Sees his passion.

                    NATASCHA
          But this is a *democracy*, Harvey.

                    DENT
          When their enemies were at the
          gate, the Romans would suspend
          democracy and appoint one man to
          protect the city.   It wasn't
          considered an honor.   It was
          considered public service.

                    RACHEL
          And the last man they asked to
          protect the republic was named
          Caesar.   He never gave up that
          power.

                    DENT
          Well, I guess you either die a hero
          or you live long enough to see
          yourself become the villain.   Look,
          whoever the Batman is, he doesn't
          want to spend the rest of his life
          doing this.   How could he? Batman's
          looking for someone to take up his
          mantle.

                    NATASCHA
          Someone like you, Mr.Dent?

                    DENT
          Maybe.   If I'm up to it.

Natascha reaches up and covers the top half of Dent's face.

                    NATASCHA
          But what if Harvey Dent *is* the
          caped crusader?

                    DENT
          If *I* were sneaking out every night
          someone would've noticed by now.

Dent takes Rachel's hand.   Rachel glances at Wayne.
Awkward.

                    WAYNE

Well, you've sold me, Dent. I'm
gonna throw you a fundraiser.

                    DENT
          That's nice of you, Bruce, but I'm
          not up for reelection for three
          years. That stuff won't start for-

                    WAYNE
          I don't think you understand. One
          fundraiser with *my* pals, you'll
          never need another cent.

EXT. BACK ALLEY, HOTEL, DOWNTOWN -- DAY

A line of high-end AUTOS dispenses well dressed GANGSTERS.

INT. KITCHEN, HOTEL -- DAY

The Chechen walks through a METAL DETECTOR manned by two
CHINESE. A lean, African-American man, 50's, is being
wanded. This is GAMBOL. He nods at the Chechen, wary.

INT. CONFERENCE ROOM, HOTEL -- CONTINUOUS

Gotham's most notorious GANGSTERS. A door opens, and two
BURLY CHINESE enter, carrying a TV. They set it down on
the end of the table.

                    CRIME BOSS
          The hell is this...?

The screen flickers to life: Lau. The room ERUPTS.

                    LAU (ON T.V.)
          Gentlemen, please. As you're all
          aware, one of our deposits was
          stolen. A relatively small amount:
          68 million.

                    CHECHEN
          Who's stupid enough steal from us?

                    LAU
          I'm told the man who arranged the
          heist calls himself Joker.

                    CHECHEN
          Who the hell is that?

                    MARONI
          Two-bit whack-job wears a cheap
          purple suit and make-up. He's not
          the problem- he's a *nobody*.
                (looks at Lau)
          The *problem* is our money being
          tracked by the cops.

Murmurs of surprise.

                    LAU
          Thanks to Mr.Maroni's well-placed
          sources we know that police have
          indeed identified our banks using
          marked bills and are planning to
          seize your funds today-

Everyone starts SHOUTING at once.

EXT. VARIOUS DOWNTOWN BANKS -- CONTINUOUS

Gordon sits in a SWAT van outside a bank. Stephens is
outside another. Ramirez a third...

SWAT teams CHECK WEAPONS and prepare move...

INT. SOCIAL CLUB, DOWNTOWN -- CONTINUOUS

Lau waits for the noise to subside.

                    CHECHEN
          You promised safe, clean money
          launder-

                    LAU
          With the investigation ongoing,
          none of you can risk hanging on to
          your own proceeds. And since the
          enthusiastic new D.A. has put all
          my competitors out of business, I'm
          your only option.

                    MARONI
          So what are you proposing?

                    LAU
          Moving all deposits to one secure
          location. Not *a bank.*

                    GAMBOL

Where, then?

                    LAU
          Obviously, no one can know but me.
          If the police were to gain leverage
          over one of you everyone's *money*
          would be at stake.

                    CHECHEN
          What stops them getting to you?

                    LAU
          As the money is moved I go to Hong
          Kong. Far from Dent's
          jurisdiction. And the Chinese will
          not extradite one of their own.

From the back of the room comes LAUGHTER. It grows and
grows, until it fills the room. All eyes turn:

The Joker. Sweaty clown makeup obscuring the AWFUL SCARS
which widen his mouth into a PERMANENT, GHOULISH SMILE.

                    THE JOKER
          I thought *I* told bad jokes.

                    GAMBOL
          Give me one reason I shouldn't have
          my boy here pull your head off.

The Joker pulls out a freshly sharpened pencil.

                    THE JOKER
          How about a magic trick?

The Joker SLAMS the pencil into the table, leaving it
UPRIGHT.

                    THE JOKER (CONT'D)
          I'll make this pencil disappear.

Gambol nods. His BODYGUARD MOVES at the Joker- who
SIDESTEPS- GRIPS his head- SLAMS it, FACE DOWN, onto the
table...

The Bodyguard goes LIMP and slides off of the table. The
PENCIL is gone. MAGIC. The Joker BOWS. Grins at Gambol.

                    THE JOKER (CONT'D)

And by the way, the suit wasn't
cheap. You should know. You
bought it.

Gambol STANDS, furious. The Chechen stops him.

                    CHECHEN
          Sit. I wanna hear proposition.

The Joker nods his thanks. Rises.

                    THE JOKER
          A year ago these cops and lawyers
          wouldn't dare cross any of you.
          What happened? Did your balls drop
          off? See, a guy like me-

                    GAMBOL
          A freak.

Laughs. Which the Joker tries to ignore.

                    THE JOKER
          A guy like me... *I* know why you're
          holding your little group therapy
          session in broad daylight. *I* know
          why you're afraid to go out at
          night. *Batman*. He's shown Gotham
          your true colors. And Dent's just
          the beginning.
               (indicates Lau)
          And as for his so-called plan-
          Batman has no *jurisdiction*. He'll
          find him and make him squeal.
               (smiles at Lau)
          I can tell the squealers every
          time.

                    CHECHEN
          What you propose?

                    THE JOKER
          It's simple. Kill the Batman.

Jeers. Laughter.

                    MARONI
          If it's so easy why haven't you
          done it already?

                         THE JOKER
            Like my mother used to tell me- if
            you're good at something, never do
            it for free.

                         CHECHEN
            How much you want?

                         THE JOKER
            Half.

Laughter. The Joker shrugs. Rises.

                         THE JOKER (CONT'D)
            You don't deal with this now, soon
            Gambol won't even be able to get a
            nickel for his grandma-

                         GAMBOL
            Enough from the clown.

Gambol gets up, MOVING at the Joker, who casually opens his
coat, revealing EXPLOSIVES wired to his chest. Gambol
stops.

                         THE JOKER
            Let's not blow this out of all
            proportion.

Gambol stares at the Joker. Hard.

                         GAMBOL
            You think you can steal from us and
            just walk away? I'm putting the
            word out- 5 hundred grand for this
            clown dead. A million alive, so I
            get to teach him some manners,
            first.

The Joker shrugs. Turns to the assembled.

                         THE JOKER
            Let me know when you change your
            minds.

The Joker strolls out. Maroni turns to Lau.

                         MARONI
            How soon can you move the money?

EXT. VARIOUS BANKS DOWNTOWN -- CONTINUOUS

Gordon hurries up the steps to a bank. SWAT teams rush the
various banks.

> LAU (O.S.)
> *I already have...*

EXT. UNDERPASS, GOTHAM -- CONTINUOUS

A CHINESE MAN finishes loading a TRACTOR TRAILER with cash
boxes. The truck pulls out into a CONVOY.

INT. BANK VAULT -- CONTINUOUS

Gordon stands in an almost empty bank vault. Furious.

> LAU (O.S.)
> *For obvious reasons I couldn't wait*
> *for your permission...*

INT. SOCIAL CLUB, DOWNTOWN -- CONTINUOUS

The shot of Lau on the TV widens...

> LAU
> Rest assured, your money is safe.

He is already on his private jet.

IN THE SKY: THE BAT SIGNAL.

EXT. ROOF, POLICE STATION -- NIGHT

Batman emerges from the shadows. The man next to the
glowing spotlight turns: DENT.

> DENT
> You're a hard man to reach.

Gordon BURSTS onto the rooftop, weapon drawn. Sees Dent.

> DENT (CONT'D)
> Lau's halfway to Hong Kong- if
> you'd *asked*, I could have taken his
> passport- I told you to keep me in
> the loop.

> GORDON

Yeah? All that was left in the
vaults were the marked bills- they
knew we were coming! As soon as
your office got involved, there's a
leak-

                    DENT
My office?! You're sitting down
here with scum like Wuertz and
Ramirez...
        (off look)
Oh, yeah, Gordon- I almost had your
rookie cold on a racketeering beef.

                    GORDON
Don't try to cloud the fact that
clearly Maroni's got people in your
office, Dent.

Dent turns to Batman.

                    DENT
We need Lau back, but the Chinese
won't extradite a national under
any circumstances.

                    BATMAN
If I get him to you, can you get
him to talk?

                    DENT
I'll get him to *sing*.

                    GORDON
We're going after the mob's life
savings. Things *will* get ugly.

                    DENT
I knew the risks when I took this
job, lieutenant. Same as you.
        (turns to Batman)
How will you get him back, anyway?

Batman is gone. Dent looks around, startled. Gordon
smirks.

                    GORDON
He does that.

INT. FOX'S OFFICE, WAYNE INDUSTRIES -- DAY

Fox gets up from behind his desk.

>   FOX
>   Our Chinese friend left town before
>   I could tell him the deal is off.

>   WAYNE
>   I'm sure you've always wanted to go
>   to Hong Kong.

Fox opens the door to a private elevator.

INT. PRIVATE ELEVATOR -- CONTINUOUS

Fox turns a key.

>   FOX
>   What's wrong with a phone call?

>   WAYNE
>   I think Mr.Lau deserves a more
>   *personal* touch.

INT. APPLIED SCIENCES DIVISION -- CONTINUOUS

Fox leads Wayne off the elevator and into the vast space.

>   FOX
>   For high altitude jumps, you need
>   oxygen and stabilizers. I must
>   say- compared to your usual
>   requests, jumping out of an
>   airplane is pretty straightforward.

Lucius stops at a cabinet, pulls open a drawer and hauls
out an oxygen tank and ribbed rubber hosing.

>   WAYNE
>   How about getting back into the
>   plane?

>   FOX
>   I can recommend a good travel
>   agent.

>   WAYNE
>   Without it landing.

                    FOX
          That's more like it, Mr.Wayne.

He shuts the drawer. Moves off, thinking.

                    FOX (CONT'D)
          I don't think I have anything here.
          The CIA had a program in the '60s
          for getting their people out of hot
          spots. Called Sky Hook. Now-

Fox opens a cabinet to reveal COMPONENTS OF A NEW BAT-SUIT.
ARMORED PLATING secured to mesh. Wayne lifts an arm.

                    FOX (CONT'D)
          Hardened kevlar plates on a
          titanium-dipped fiber tri-weave for
          flexibility...

Wayne examines DOUBLE BLADE SCALLOPS on the gauntlet...

                    FOX (CONT'D)
          You'll be lighter, faster, more
          agile...

Wayne flinches as the BLADES FIRE, SPINNING LIKE THROWING
STARS, NARROWLY MISSING his ear, embedding themselves in a
filing cabinet. Fox looks at him.

                    FOX (CONT'D)
          Perhaps you should read the
          instructions, first.

                    WAYNE
          Sorry.

Fox picks up the chest, demonstrating its flexibility.

                    FOX
          Now, there's a trade-off... the
          spread of the plates gives you weak
          spots. You'll be more vulnerable
          to gunfire and knives.

                    WAYNE
          We wouldn't want things getting too
          easy, would we?
               (picks up suit)
          How will it hold up against dogs?

Fox looks at him quizzically.

>   FOX
>   You talking chihuahuas or
>   rotweilers?
>   (Wayne smiles)
>   It should do fine against *cats*.

INT. BAT-BUNKER -- DAY

Wayne examines a parachute harness. Alfred unfolds a
diagram of a NAVY CARGO PLANE with a giant "V" mounted on
the front.

>   ALFRED
>   I found one. In Arizona. Very
>   nice man says it will take him a
>   week to get it running. And he
>   takes cash. What about a flight
>   crew?

>   WAYNE
>   South Korean smugglers. They run
>   flights into Pyongyang, below radar
>   the whole way. Did you think of an
>   alibi?

Alfred looks quite pleased with himself.

>   ALFRED
>   Oh, yes.

EXT. BALLET -- NIGHT

Rachel and Dent arrive to find the box office SHUTTERED. A
sign:'PERFORMANCE CANCELED.' A newspaper story is taped to
the glass. Over a picture of BRUCE WAYNE ON A YACHT:

LOVE BOAT- Billionaire absconds with entire Moscow ballet.

EXT. DECK, WAYNE'S YACHT, THE CARIBBEAN -- DAY

Alfred, picks his way over twelve SUNBATHING BALLERINAS.
Wayne looks up from a newspaper. Alfred points to a SEA-
PLANE gently touching down across the bay.

>   ALFRED
>   I believe your plane is here.

>   WAYNE

You look tired, Alfred. Will you
be all right without me?

A Ballerina rolls over- waves the suntan lotion at Alfred.

               ALFRED
If you can tell me the Russian for
'apply your own bloody suntan
lotion.'

Wayne tosses a large, waterproof kit bag into the water and
JUMPS in after it. Begins swimming over to the sea-plane.

INT. POOL HALL -- NIGHT

Gambol racks up. A bodyguard steps into the room.

              BODYGUARD
Somebody here for you.

Gambol looks to the back- three rough customers are
waiting.

            BODYGUARD (CONT'D)
They say they've killed the Joker.
They've come for the reward.

               GAMBOL
They bring proof?

              BODYGUARD
They say they've brought the body.

The bodyguards FLOP a BODY wrapped in garbage bags onto the
table. The BOUNTY HUNTERS wait in the corner. Gambol
pulls back one of the garbage bags, revealing the Joker's
bloodied face. Gambol spits. Turns to face the bounty
hunters.

               GAMBOL
So. *Dead* you get five hundred-

Behind Gambol, the Joker SITS UP- THRUSTS knives into the
bodyguards' chests. Gambol spins to see a crazy grin on
the Joker's spit-dribbled face-

             THE JOKER
How about alive?

The Joker gets a switchblade in Gambol's mouth- SHARP METAL PULLING THE CHEEK TAUT. The Bounty Hunters subdue the remaining bodyguards.

>   THE JOKER (CONT'D)
>   Wanna know how I got these scars?
>   My father was a drinker and a
>   fiend. He'd beat mommy right in
>   front of me. One night he goes off
>   crazier than usual, mommy gets the
>   kitchen knife to defend herself.
>   He doesn't like that. Not. One.
>   Bit.

The Joker TUGS Gambols cheek with the blade.

>   THE JOKER (CONT'D)
>   So, me watching, he takes the knife
>   to her, laughing while he does it.
>   Turns to me and says 'why so
>   serious?' Comes at me with the
>   knife- 'why so serious?' Sticks
>   the blade in my mouth- 'Let's put a
>   *smile* on that face' and...

The Joker looks up at the ASHEN FACES of the remaining Body Guards. Smiles.

>   THE JOKER (CONT'D)
>   Why so serious?

The Joker FLICKS his wrist- the Body Guards flinch as Gambol goes down. The Joker turns to them.

>   THE JOKER (CONT'D)
>   Now, our organization is small, but
>   we've got a lot of potential for
>   aggressive expansion... so which of
>   you fine gentlemen would like to
>   join our team?

The three bodyguards all nod. The Joker SNAPS a pool cue.

>   THE JOKER (CONT'D)
>   Only one slot open right now- so
>   we're going to have try-outs.

The Joker drops the broken cue in the middle of the men.

                    THE JOKER (CONT'D)
          Make it fast.

The men stare at each other.   Then at the jagged pool cue.

EXT.PENINSULA HOTEL, HONG KONG -- DAY

A HELICOPTER touches down on one of the hotel's twin
helipads. Two L.S.I. VPs approach, heads ducked. Fox gets
out- they shake hands, shouting over the engine-

                    VP
          Welcome to Hong Kong, Mr.Fox!
          Mr.Lau regrets he is unable to meet
          you in person. But with his
          current legal difficulties...!

                    FOX
          I understand!

INT. LOBBY, L.S.I.HOLDINGS -- DAY

The VPs usher Fox towards security.

                    VP
          I'm afraid for security reasons I
          have to ask for your mobile phone.

Lucius hands his phone to a SECURITY GUARD, who puts the
phone in a box underneath his station.

INT. L.S.I.HOLDINGS -- DAY

Fox and Lau eat lunch in a dining room overlooking the
city.

                    LAU
          I must apologize for leaving Gotham
          in the middle of our negotiations.
          This *misunderstanding* with the
          Gotham police force... I couldn't
          let such a thing threaten my
          company. A businessman of your
          stature will understand. But with
          you here... we can continue.

                    FOX
          Well, it was good of you to bring
          me out here in such style, Mr.Lau.
          But I've actually come...

A CELL PHONE rings. Fox pulls out a second, identical,
phone. Fox presses the off switch and places the phone by
his plate.

                    LAU
          We do not allow cell phones in-

                    FOX
          Sorry. Forgot I had it. So, I've
          come to explain why we're going to
          have to put our deal *on hold*...

Lau stares at Fox. Clearly furious. Fox smiles.

                    FOX (CONT'D)
          We can't afford to be seen to do
          business with... well, whatever it
          is you're accused of being. A
          businessman of your stature will
          understand.

Lau gets up. Silent. Fox retrieves his phone. Stands.

                    LAU
              (cold)
          I think, Mr.Fox, that a simple
          phone call might have sufficed.

                    FOX
          Well, I do *love* Chinese food. And
          Mr.Wayne didn't want you to think
          we'd been deliberately wasting your
          time.

                    LAU
          Just accidentally wasting it.

                    FOX
              (laughs)
          That's very good- "accidentally".
          Very good. I'll be sure and tell
          Mr.Wayne that he was wrong about
          you not having a sense of humor.

INT. LOBBY, L.S.I.HOLDINGS -- DAY

Lucius walks back through security. Nods at the VP, who
bows, offering Lucius his cell phone. Lucius shakes his

head, holds up the IDENTICAL PHONE. The VP smiles, nods,
puts the phone back into the tray with several others.

INT. HOLD, C-130 CARGO HAULER -- DAWN

Two SMUGGLERS steal glances at Wayne, crouched at the rear
in balaclava and flight suit. The COPILOT signals Wayne,
who pulls on his oxygen mask and stands up. The rear of
the plane OPENS. Wayne steps to the edge, then JUMPS.

EXT. SKIES ABOVE HONG KONG -- DAWN

Moving across the water towards Hong Kong harbor...

A tiny figure DROPS into frame, PLUMMETING towards the
water- SPEEDING past the highest floors of skyscrapers,
seconds from impact. Wayne PULLS the chute- DROPS into the
water...

EXT. BENEATH FREEWAY, HONG KONG HARBOR -- DAY

Wayne pulls himself out of the water, dragging up his pack.

EXT. CENTRAL ESCALATORS -- DAY

Wayne stops halfway up the crowded commuter escalator. He
takes a camera and lines up a shot like any tourist.

                    FOX (O.S.)
          There's a better view from the peak
          tram.

Wayne turns to find Fox standing there, street map out.

                    WAYNE
          How's the view from L.S.I.Holdings?

                    FOX
          Restricted. Lau's holed up in
          there good and tight. Here...

Fox shows Wayne the phone. The display: *a 3-d map of Lau's
office suite.* Wayne takes the phone, impressed.

                    WAYNE
          What's this?

                    FOX
          I had R and D work it up- it sends
          out high frequencies and records

                    the response time to map an
                    environment.

                              WAYNE
                         (smiles)
                    Sonar. Just like a b-

                              FOX
                    Submarine. Like a submarine.

                              WAYNE
                    And the other device?

                              FOX
                    In place.

Wayne nods, moves away.

                              FOX (CONT'D)
                    Mr.Wayne?
                         (Wayne turns)
                    Good luck.

EXT. HONG KONG -- NIGHT

Moving towards the tallest building in the glittering
skyline to find Wayne, crouched on the roof. The blades of
his gauntlets CLICK into place. He dons the helmet-like
cowl. His "cape" is in the form of a hard faceted PACK.

He stands- pulls two black boxes from his belt, CLICKS them
together and UNFOLDS them into a RIFLE-LIKE DEVICE. Batman
SCOPES a second, lower building. Adjust a setting and
FIRES- four times...

Four small STICKY BOMBS SLAP onto the glass of the lower
building. They have visible timers which are COUNTING
DOWN.

INT. LOBBY, L.S.I.HOLDINGS -- NIGHT

Lucius' cell phone GLOWS in the box under the Security
Guard's desk. CHARACTERS race across the screen.

Then the monitor FLICKERS off, the lights DIM and all of
the security doors in the front of the building OPEN at
once.

The Guard grabs his radio- CALLS FOR HELP...

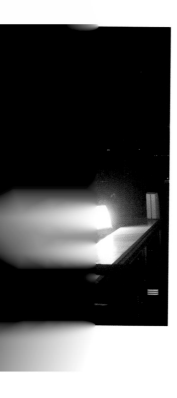

EXT. ROOFTOP OVERLOOKING L.S.I.HOLDINGS

Batman LAUNCHES into the glittering night, DROPPING from
the tall tower... his pack BURSTS OPEN, becoming his BAT
WINGS-he GLIDES down to the lower building, STREAKING
around it, BANKING HARD to line up with a window in the
rear...

INT. LAU'S OFFICE, L.S.I.HOLDINGS -- NIGHT

Lau is talking on the phone, staring at a profit projection
on a flat screen monitor. Suddenly the room goes dark.

EXT. L.S.I.HOLDINGS -- CONTINUOUS

As Batman HURTLES towards the glass he COLLAPSES his wings,
WRAPPING his cape around himself and CANNONBALLING THROUGH
THE GLASS-

INT. LAU'S OFFICE SUITE, L.S.I.HOLDINGS -- NIGHT

-ROLLING across the floor in a flurry of broken glass...

INT. LAU'S OFFICE, TOP FLOOR, L.S.I.HOLDINGS -- NIGHT

Lau pulls out a HANDGUN.

INT. HALLWAY, L.S.I.HOLDINGS -- NIGHT

Lau steps into the hallway. His BODYGUARDS are waiting for
him, carrying FLASHLIGHTS.

                    LAU (IN CHINESE)
          Where the hell are the cops?

                         BODYGUARD (IN CHINESE)
              Coming.

                    LAU (IN CHINESE)
              What the hell am I paying them for?

They head for the stairwell.

EXT. L.S.I.HOLDINGS -- NIGHT

A small ARMY of Hong Kong police lead by a HONG KONG
DETECTIVE descends on the building.

INT. MEZZANINE LEVEL, L.S.I.HOLDINGS -- NIGHT

Lau and his men make their way out onto the mezzanine.

Across the room, something makes a CRASHING SOUND. Lau's men fan out, trying to cover the room with their flashlights.

Suddenly, one of the flashlights goes DARK. Then another. Someone SCREAMS.

Lau FIRES. Then FIRES again. The muzzle flash from his weapon STROBES the room.

EXT. L.S.I.HOLDINGS, HONG KONG -- NIGHT

Cops SWARM into the building. A LOBBY SECURITY GUARD directs the Hong Kong Detective where to go...

INT. OFFICE, L.S.I.HOLDINGS -- NIGHT

Lau LOCKS the door. RELOADS. The door is KICKED open. Lau FIRES. No one is there.

Lau stares, finger restless on the trigger. From his right- a NOISE. He turns and FIRES.

In the muzzle FLASH: Batman, bearing down on him like a demon.

Lau FIRES, and FIRES again as Batman TACKLES him. Batman pulls out a SMALL PACK- STRAPS it onto Lau-

The COUNTER on the sticky bombs hits 0-

The Hong Kong Detective and the Cops BURST into the room- the WALL AND CEILING BEHIND BATMAN AND LAU EXPLODES- revealing the dawn sky above Hong Kong.

The Detective looks around as he hears a LOW RUMBLE...

Batman JERKS the RIPCORD on Lau's pack. Cops cower as a WEATHER BALLOON EXPLODES out of the pack, unreeling high- test nylon. The Cops cock their weapons.

Lau looks up. Bemused. The weather balloon is two hundred feet up, swaying gently. The RUMBLE BUILDS...

Suddenly, a MASSIVE C-130 ROARS over. The large V on the front of the plane SNAGS the line- Lau and BATMAN are YANKED THROUGH THE HOLE IN THE CEILING-

Lau SCREAMS as he and Batman SOAR UP INTO THE DAWN SKY...

The Detective looks up. Batman and Lau are gone.

INT. GORDON'S OFFICE, MCU, GOTHAM CENTRAL -- DAY

Gordon is looking through case files. Ramirez walks in.

               RAMIREZ
     You're gonna want to see this.

EXT. MCU -- DAY

Gordon follows Ramirez through a CROWD of excited cops. On
the ground, trussed like a chicken- Lau. A sign taped to
his chest: 'Please deliver to Lieutenant Gordon.'

INT. INTERROGATION ROOM, MCU, GOTHAM CENTRAL -- DAY

Lau sits next to his sleazy lawyer, EVANS. Rachel walks
in.

               RACHEL
     Give us the money and we'll deal.

               LAU
     The *money* is the only reason I'm
     still alive.

Rachel leans forward, speaking softly. Clearly.

               RACHEL
     You mean when they hear that you've
     helped us they're going to kill
     you?

               EVANS
     Are you *threatening* my client?

               RACHEL
     No, I'm just assuming your client's
     cooperation with this
     investigation. *As will everyone.*
         (moves to the door)
     Enjoy your stay in County, Mr.Lau.

               LAU
     Wait.
         (Rachel stops)

                    I won't give you the money, but
                    I'll give you my clients. All of
                    them.

                              RACHEL
                    You were a glorified accountant-
                    what could you have on *all* of them
                    that we could charge?

                              LAU
                    I'm good with calculation- I
                    handled all their investments. One
                    big pot.

INT. OBSERVATION ROOM, MCU, GOTHAM CENTRAL -- DAY

Dent hits a buzzer. Turns to Gordon.

                              DENT
                    I've got it. RICO. If their money
                    was *pooled* we can charge all of
                    them as one criminal conspiracy.

                              GORDON
                    Charge them with what?

Rachel enters.

                              DENT
                    In a RICO case if we can charge *any*
                    of the conspirators with a felony-

                              RACHEL
                    We can charge *all* of them with it.

Dent nods at Rachel, excited.

INT. INTERROGATION ROOM, MCU, GOTHAM CENTRAL -- DAY

Rachel comes back in.

                              RACHEL
                    Mr.Lau, do you have details of this
                    communal fund? Ledgers,
                    notebooks...?

                              LAU
                         (smiles)
                    Immunity, protection and a
                    chartered plane back to Hong Kong.

                    RACHEL
          Once you've testified in open
          court. So with your clients locked
          up, what happens to all that money?

                    LAU
          Like I said- I'm good with
          calculation.

INT. OBSERVATION ROOM, MCU, GOTHAM CENTRAL -- CONTINUOUS

Dent and Gordon watch Lau.

                    GORDON
          He can't go to County. I'll keep
          him here in the holding cells.

                    DENT
          What is this Gordon, your fortress?

                    GORDON
          You trust them over at County?

                    DENT
          I don't trust them *here*.

                    GORDON
          Lau stays.

                    DENT
          It's your call, Lieutenant. Be
          right.

                    GORDON
          I am, counselor.

EXT. CITY HALL -- DAY

Dent stands in front of a small crowd of reporters.

                    REPORTER
          The Chinese government claim their
          international rights have been
          broken.

                    DENT
          I don't know about Mr. Lau's travel
          arrangements...

INT. RESTAURANT -- CONTINUOUS

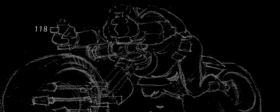

Dent's press conference plays on a TV in the corner.

> DENT
> (*grins*)
> *...but I'm sure glad he's back.*

Maroni and the Chechen are watching the TV.

> CHECHEN
> I put word out. We hire the clown.
> (off look)
> He was right. We have to fix real
> problem. Batman.

Maroni shakes his head. Spots Gordon walking over dangling
a pair of handcuffs. Nods at the TV.

> GORDON
> Our boy looks good on the tube.

> MARONI
> You sure you want to embarrass me
> in front of my friends, Lieutenant?

> GORDON
> Don't worry, they're coming, too.

Gordon points out the window to a PRISON BUS.

EXT. VARIOUS DOWNTOWN AND OUTLYING LOCATIONS -- DAY

Prison buses in every neighborhood. COPS load them with
CRIMINALS. Stephens puts Crime Boss in a prison bus.

INT. COURTROOM A, GOTHAM MUNICIPAL COURTHOUSE -- DAY

JUDGE SURRILLO reads the list of charges.

> JUDGE SURRILLO
> ...849 counts racketeering, 246
> counts fraud, 87 counts conspiracy
> murder...

Judge Surrillo turns the page. A PLAYING CARD sits there.
A Joker. He glances at it, curious, puts it to one side.

> JUDGE SURRILLO (CONT'D)
> ...how do the defendants plead?

An ARMY of DEFENSE LAWYERS jostle YELLING ALL AT ONCE. The
STENOGRAPHER looks up, helpless.

INT. MAYOR'S OFFICE -- DAY

The MAYOR, COMMISSIONER LOEB, and Gordon look up as Dent
enters.

                    MAYOR
          DENT! What was that circus?!

                    DENT
          I asked Gordon to make some
          arrests.

                    LOEB
               (looks at report)
          Five hundred and-

                    GORDON
          Forty-nine, sir.

Gordon nods at Dent, approving. Dent grins back.

                    MAYOR
          549 criminals at once?! How did
          you convince Surrillo to hear this
          farce?

                    DENT
          She shares my enthusiasm for
          justice. After all, she is a
          judge.

                    MAYOR
          Even if you blow enough smoke to
          get convictions out of Surrillo,
          you'll set a new record at appeals
          for quickest kick in the ass.

                    DENT
          It won't matter. The head guys
          make bail, sure... but the *mid-
          level guys*, they can't, and they
          can't afford to be off the streets
          long enough for trial and appeal.
          They'll cut deals that include some
          jail time. Think of all you could
          do with *18 months* of clean streets.

The Mayor waves Gordon and Loeb out.

>   MAYOR
>   The public likes you, Dent. That's
>   the *only* reason this might fly.
>   But that means it's on *you*.
>   They're *all* coming after you, now.
>   Not just the mob... politicians,
>   journalists, cops- anyone whose
>   wallet's about to get lighter. Are
>   you up to it?
>   (Dent smiles)
>   You better be. They get anything
>   on you... those criminals will be
>   back on the streets...

The Mayor turns to look out of the window. Quiet.

>   MAYOR (CONT'D)
>   Followed swiftly by you and me-

BANG! A DARK SHAPE CRACKS THE GLASS in front of the
Mayor's nose. Dent rushes to the window, looks out...

EXT. CITY HALL -- CONTINUOUS

PEDESTRIANS look up, someone SCREAMS, someone POINTS- five
stories up... SWINGING from a FLAGPOLE...

BATMAN. HANGING BY HIS NECK. DEAD. His mouth roughly
painted in a DEMONIC CLOWN SMILE.

EXT. CITY HALL -- MOMENTS LATER

"Batman" is lowered from the flagpole. The same fake
Batman we saw earlier. Pinned to his chest by a KNIFE, a
PLAYING CARD. A Joker. Gordon moves closer to the body.
The card has writing on it: ***WILL THE REAL BATMAN PLEASE
STAND UP?***

INT. WAYNE PENTHOUSE -- DAY

Wayne comes into the living room, excited. Alfred is
supervising party arrangements.

>   WAYNE
>   How's it going?

>   ALFRED

I think your fundraiser will be a
great success, sir.

            WAYNE
And why do you think I wanted to
hold a party for Harvey Dent?

            ALFRED
I assumed it was your usual reason
for socialising beyond myself and
the scum of Gotham's underbelly: to
try and impress Miss Dawes.

            WAYNE
Very droll. But very wrong.
Actually it's Dent. You see-

Wayne trails off as he spots something on the television:
the Batman HANGING as from a NEWS CAMERA, framed by a
graphic that reads **'BATMAN DEAD?'**. *Image cuts to Engel in*
the studio.

            ENGEL (V.O.)
...Police released video footage
found concealed on the body.
Sensitive viewers be aware: it is
disturbing.

The image cuts to a BLINDFOLDED MAN, wearing a makeshift
Batman costume- face bruised and bloody. In some kind of
bright, fluorescent-lit room.

            VOICE (O.S.)
Tell them your name.

            MAN
        (*weak*)
Brian Douglas.

            VOICE (O.S.)
Are you the real Batman?

            MAN
No.

            VOICE (O.S.)
Why do you dress up like him?

            MAN

He's a symbol... that we don't have
to be afraid of scum like you...

> VOICE (O.S.)
> But you **do**, Brian. You really do.
> You think the Batman's helped
> Gotham?

Brian nods uncertainly...

> VOICE (CONT'D)
> Look at me.
>   (Brian looks down)
> LOOK AT ME!

Brian looks up- the camera swings into the face of the
Joker, in CHALK-WHITE makeup, RED SMEAR of lipstick on his
SCARS.

> THE JOKER
> This is how crazy Batman's made
> Gotham. You want order in Gotham?
> Batman has to go. So...
>   (leans in)
> Batman must take off his mask, and
> turn himself in. Every day he
> doesn't... people will die.
> Starting tonight. I'm a man of my
> word.

The tape cuts to STATIC.

Wayne turns to Alfred. Silent.

INT. WAYNE PENTHOUSE -- EVENING

Dent and Rachel get off the lift. Dent stands in awe of
the penthouse and its guests.

> RACHEL
> Now I've seen it all: Harvey Dent,
> scourge of the underworld, scared
> stiff by the trust fund brigade.

Rachel spots someone and darts off-

> DENT
> Rachel-

> ALFRED (O.S.)

A little liquid courage, Mr.Dent?

Dent turns to see Alfred with drinks on a silver tray.

> DENT
> Thanks. Alfred, right?

> ALFRED
> Yes, sir.

> DENT
> Rachel talks about you all the
> time. You've known her her whole
> life?

> ALFRED
> Not yet, sir.

> DENT
> (smiles, surveys
> crowd)
> Any psychotic ex-boyfriends I
> should be aware of?

> ALFRED
> Oh, you have *no* idea.

Alfred leaves Dent standing there, puzzled. The crowd
REACTS as a LOUD ROAR drowns conversation... Dent looks
out-

EXT. HELIPAD, WAYNE PENTHOUSE -- CONTINUOUS

Wayne's CHOPPER touches down. He spills out with a clutch
of SUPERMODELS...

INT. WAYNE PENTHOUSE -- CONTINUOUS

Wayne and the supermodels come out of the helipad elevator-

> WAYNE
> Sorry, I'm late- glad you started
> without me! Where's Rachel?!

Rachel cringes slightly. Wayne spots her.

> WAYNE (CONT'D)
> *Rachel Dawes*- my oldest friend.
> When she told me she was dating
> Harvey Dent, I had one thing to

say... the guy from those god-
awful campaign commercials?

Laughter. Dent shifts, embarrassed.

> WAYNE (CONT'D)
> 'I Believe in Harvey Dent.' Nice
> slogan, Harvey. Certainly caught
> Rachel's attention. But then I
> started paying attention to Harvey,
> and all he's been doing as our new
> D.A., and you know what? *I* believe
> in Harvey Dent. On his watch,
> Gotham can feel a little safer. A
> little more optimistic. So get out
> your checkbooks and let's make sure
> that he stays right where all of
> Gotham wants him...
> (raises his glass)
> All except Gotham's criminals, of
> course. To the face of Gotham's
> bright future- Harvey Dent.

Dent smiles accepting the toast.

INT. CORRIDOR, MCU -- EVENING

Ramirez catches up to Gordon, holding paperwork.

> RAMIREZ
> That Joker card pinned to the body?
> Forensics found three sets of
> D.N.A..

> GORDON
> Any matches?

> RAMIREZ
> All three.

Gordon STOPS. Turns to face her.

> RAMIREZ (CONT'D)
> The D.N.A. belongs to Judge
> Surrillo, Harvey Dent and
> Commissioner Loeb.

> GORDON

The Joker's telling us who he's
targeting- get a unit to Surrillo's
house, tell Wuertz to find Dent-
get them both into protective
custody. Where's the Commissioner?

> RAMIREZ
> City hall.

> GORDON
> Seal the building. *No one* in or
> out till I get there.

EXT. DECK, WAYNE'S PENTHOUSE -- EVENING

Wayne walks out to the edge of the balcony and looks over
Gotham. Hears someone behind him- Rachel.

> RACHEL
> Harvey may not know you well enough
> to understand when you're making
> fun of him. But I do.

> WAYNE
> (shakes his head)
> I meant every word.

Wayne moves closer to Rachel. Takes her arm.

> WAYNE (CONT'D)
> The day you once told me about, the
> day when Gotham no longer needs
> Batman. It's coming.

Rachel looks at Wayne. Conflicted. He moves closer.

> RACHEL
> You can't ask me to wait for that.

Wayne takes Rachel's arms, looking at her, excited.

> WAYNE
> It's happening *now*- Harvey *is* that
> hero. He locked up half the city's
> criminals, and he did it without
> wearing a mask. Gotham *needs* a
> hero with a face.

> DENT (O.S.)

                    You can throw a party, Wayne, I'll
                    give you that. Thanks again. Mind
                    if I borrow Rachel?

Rachel glances back at Wayne as she moves to Dent. Wayne
watches them head inside.

EXT. STREET, GOTHAM HEIGHTS -- EVENING

Two MEN in suits knock at a Brownstone. The door is opened
by Judge Surrillo. The two Men hold up BADGES.

EXT. CITY HALL -- EVENING

Gordon enters through a tight police presence at the doors.

INT. POLICE COMMISSIONER'S OFFICE -- EVENING

Gordon enters to find Loeb, flanked by armed cops.

                    COMMISSIONER LOEB
                Gordon, what are you playing at?

Gordon checks the window. Turns to his men.

                    GORDON
                We're secure. I want a floor-by-
                floor search of the entire
                building.
                    (turns to Loeb)
                I'm sorry, sir. We believe the
                Joker has made a threat against
                your life.

                    LOEB
                Gordon, you're unlikely to discover
                this for yourself, so take my word-
                the Police Commissioner earns a lot
                of threats...

Loeb pulls a bottle of whisky and a tumbler from a drawer.

                    LOEB (CONT'D)
                I found the appropriate response to
                these situations a long time ago...

EXT. STREET, GOTHAM HEIGHTS -- EVENING

The second man is waiting by the Judge's car.

                         SURRILLO
              Gordon wants me to go right now?

                         MAN 1
              These are dangerous people, Judge.
              Even we don't know where you're
              going.

He hands Surrillo a sealed envelope. Opens the car door.

                         MAN 2
              Get in, then open the envelope.
              It'll tell you where you're headed.

Surrillo climbs in. Watches them drive away. She opens
the envelope- pulls out a sheet of paper. One word on it:

'UP'.

Surrillo's car EXPLODES, heaving the car upwards on a
FIREBALL.

A PASSERBY is thrown to the ground. After a moment,
BURNING DEBRIS flutters down on him. PLAYING CARDS.
JOKERS.

INT. POLICE COMMISSIONER'S OFFICE -- CONTINUOUS

Loeb pours himself a glass of whisky.

                         LOEB
              You get to explain to my wife why
              I'm late for dinner, Lieutenant.

                         GORDON
              Sir, the Joker card had a trace of
              your D.N.A. on it-

A bang at the door. Gordon pulls his weapon, then opens
it.

                         STEPHENS
              Just the normal number of bad guys
              in the building- and they're all
              city employees. Here's a list.

                         LOEB
              How'd they get my D.N.A.?

Gordon looks at Stephens's list.

                              GORDON
                    Somebody with access to your house
                    or office must've lifted a tissue
                    or a glass...

Gordon, realizing, spins around-

                              GORDON (CONT'D)
                    Wait-

But Loeb is already CHOKING- he DROPS his tumbler onto the
desk- the spilled whiskey is SMOKING, eating into the wood.

                              GORDON (CONT'D)
                    Get a medic!

Loeb COLLAPSES.

OMITTED::104

OMITTED

INT. KITCHEN, WAYNE PENTHOUSE -- EVENING

Dent pulls Rachel into the kitchen, away from the crowd.

                              DENT
                    You *cannot* leave me on my own with
                    these people.

                              RACHEL
                    The whole mob's after you and
                    you're worried about these guys?

                              DENT
                    Compared to this, the mob doesn't
                    scare me. Although, I will say:
                    them gunning for you makes you see
                    things clearly.

                              RACHEL
                    Oh, yeah?

                              DENT
                    Yeah. It makes you think about
                    what you couldn't stand losing.
                    And who you want to spend the rest
                    of your life with...

Rachel looks at Dent. Smiles.

                    RACHEL
          The rest of your life, huh? That's
          a pretty big commitment.

                    DENT
          Not if the mob has their way.

                    RACHEL
          Don't.

                    DENT
          Okay. Let's be serious. What's
          your answer?

Rachel looks at him.

                    RACHEL
          I don't have an answer.

INT.LIVING ROOM, PENTHOUSE -- NIGHT

Half the guests are on their cell phones. An ASSISTANT DA
turns to his COLLEAGUE.

                    ASSISTANT DA
          Surrillo *and* Loeb?

There is a KNOCK at the front door. Alfred opens it it
find Detective Wuertz, who holds up his badge. Alfred
beckons him in- there is a SHOTGUN at the back of his head
held by-

The Joker- purple suit, make up. With friends. The Joker
SMASHES Wuertz over the head- steps over him, RACKING the
shotgun.

                    THE JOKER
          Good evening. We're the
          entertainment.

INT. KITCHEN, WAYNE PENTHOUSE -- NIGHT

Rachel is looking at Dent. Torn.

                    DENT
          I guess no answer isn't "no".

                    RACHEL
          I'm sorry, Harvey. I just...

                         DENT
              It's someone else, isn't it?

Wayne is moving up behind him. Fast-

                         DENT (CONT'D)
              Just tell me it's not Wayne. The
              guy's a complete-

Rachel's eyes go wide as Wayne puts Dent in a SLEEPER HOLD-

                         RACHEL
              What are you doing?!

Dent SLUMPS, unconscious in Wayne's arms.

                         WAYNE
              They've come for him.

From the main room- A SHOTGUN BLAST followed by SCREAMS.
Wayne stuffs Dent in a closet- puts a mop through the
handles. Rushes past Rachel-

                         WAYNE (CONT'D)
              Stay hidden.

INT. LIVING ROOM, WAYNE'S PENTHOUSE -- NIGHT

The Joker and his THUGS pour into the room, weapons raised.

INT. HALLWAY, WAYNE PENTHOUSE -- NIGHT

A THUG appears in front of Wayne, toting a shotgun.

                         THUG
              Hands up, pretty boy.

Wayne FLIPS the shotgun around in the man's hands- uses it
as a fulcrum to SNAP his forearm- SMASHES him in the jaw
with the stock without breaking step, field stripping the
shotgun and tossing the pieces in different directions.

INT. LIVING ROOM, WAYNE'S PENTHOUSE -- NIGHT

The Joker moves through the terrified guests. Smiling.

                         THE JOKER
              I only have one question: where is
              Harvey Dent?
                   (silence)

I'll settle for his loved ones...

A distinguished Gentleman steps into the Joker's path.

                    GENTLEMAN
          We're not intimidated by thugs.

The Joker stops. Stares at the man. SMILES
AFFECTIONATELY.

                    THE JOKER
          You know, you remind me of my
          father.
               (GRABS him)
          I hated my father.

The Joker has his blade in the Gentleman's mouth.

                    RACHEL (O.S.)
          Stop!

The Joker drops the Gentleman. Turns to Rachel.

                    THE JOKER
          Hello, beautiful. You must be
          Harvey's squeeze.
               (runs his knife
                across her cheek)
          And you are beautiful. You look
          nervous- it's the scars isn't it?
          Wanna know how I got them? I had a
          wife, beautiful like you. Who
          tells me I worry too much. Who
          says I need to smile more. Who
          gambles. And gets in *deep* with the
          sharks. One day they carve her
          face, and we've got no money for
          surgeries. She can't take it.
               (presses knife into
                her cheek)
          I just want to see her smile again.
          I just want her to know I don't
          care about the scars. So I put a
          razor in my mouth and do this to
          myself... And you know what?
               (starts laughing)
          She can't stand the sight of me...
               (or crying)

> She leaves! See, now I see the
> funny side. Now I'm always
> smiling.

INT. MASTER BEDROOM, WAYNE PENTHOUSE -- NIGHT

Wayne walks in. A COUPLE are hastily putting themselves
back together, alerted by the noise.

> MALE GUEST
> What's going on out there, Wayne?

Wayne doesn't answer. He walks into a closet and pulls at
a FALSE WALL. Wayne steps into the safe room.

> FEMALE GUEST
> Thank god- you've got a panic room.

The door SLAMS shut and seals with a HISS.

> MALE GUEST
> Wait! You can't-

> FEMALE GUEST
> You've got to be kidding me.

INT. LIVING ROOM, WAYNE'S PENTHOUSE -- NIGHT

The Joker raises his knife from Rachel's cheek. She SLUGS
him. He smiles.

> THE JOKER
> A little fight in you. I like
> that.

> BATMAN (O.S.)
> Then you're going to love me.

The Joker turns. Batman catches him with a BLOW, spins him
down and DISARMS him- the Joker's men jump him- Batman
takes them out two at a time- DISARMING thugs- BREAKING
forearms- the Joker CLICKS a BLADE from the toe of his shoe
and KICKS- JABBING BETWEEN THE PLATES OF ARMOR covering
Batman's ribcage-

Batman HURLS the Joker across the room. One of the Joker's
men LUNGES- Batman lays him out cold.

The Joker has another knife pressed to Rachel's neck.

                    BATMAN (CONT'D)
          Drop the knife.

                    THE JOKER
          Sure. Just take off your mask and
          show us all who you are...

Rachel shakes her head at Batman. The Joker raises his
shotgun to the side and BLOWS OUT the pane of glass next to
him. The Joker dangles Rachel out the window.

                    BATMAN
          Let her go.

                    THE JOKER
               (laughs)
          Very poor choice of words...

He lets her DROP- Rachel falls onto a SLOPING GLASS ROOF-
sliding towards the edge Batman DIVES after her-

OMITTED

EXT. BUILDING -- NIGHT

They DROP- Batman FIRES his grapple, SNAGGING Rachel's
ankle- activates one wing of his cape- They SPIN and SLOW-
Batman envelopes Rachel- they SLAM into the hood of a
passing taxi.

INT. TAXI -- CONTINUOUS

The DRIVER SCREAMS as Batman and Rachel hit the roof- ROLL
down the windshield- onto the pavement. Alive.

INT. CAR -- CONTINUOUS

The Joker looks back as his car SPEEDS away. He's
breathing hard, EXHILARATED. He touches the blood running
down his sweaty white makeup. SMACKS the back of the
driver's seat-

                    DRIVER
          What do we do about Dent?

                    THE JOKER
          I'm a man of my word.

EXT. TAXI -- CONTINUOUS

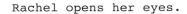

Rachel opens her eyes.

                    BATMAN
        Are you alright?

                    RACHEL
        Let's not do that again, okay?
            (looks around)
        Is Harvey-?

                    BATMAN
        He's safe.

Rachel lies back, breathing. Looks up at Batman.

                    RACHEL
        Thank you.

INT. MAJOR CRIMES UNIT, GOTHAM CENTRAL -- DAY

STEPHENS is talking to Gordon, subdued.

                  STEPHENS
        Jim, it's over.

                    GORDON
        As long as they don't get to Lau,
        we've cut off their funds.

                  STEPHENS
        But the prosecution's over.

              STEPHENS (CONT'D)
        No-one's standing up in front of a
        Judge while judges and police
        commissioners are getting blown
        away.

                    GORDON
        What about Dent?

                  STEPHENS
        If he's got any sense, Dent's
        halfway to Mexico by now.

The door BURSTS OPEN. Dent. Fire in his eyes.

                    DENT
        So where do you keep your trash?

Gordon looks at Dent. Impressed.

INT. SPECIAL HOLDING AREA, MCU, GOTHAM CENTRAL -- DAY

Lau looks up as Dent walks in, holding a bullet proof vest.

>   DENT
>   You're due in court- I need you
>   alive long enough to get you on the
>   record.

>   LAU
>   No way. You can't protect me- you
>   can't even protect *yourselves*.

Dent THROWS the heavy vest at Lau.

>   DENT
>   Refuse to cooperate on the stand-
>   you won't be coming back here-
>   you'll go to county. How long do
>   you *calculate* you'll last in there?

INT. BAT-BUNKER -- DAY

Wayne sits at his video screens- they all play the Joker's
video with different IMAGE TREATMENTS and SOUND TUNINGS.
Wayne turns to Alfred. Indicates the screens.

>   WAYNE
>   Targeting me won't get their money
>   back. I knew the mob wouldn't go
>   down without a fight, but this is
>   different. They've crossed a line.

>   ALFRED
>   You crossed it first, sir. You've
>   hammered them, squeezed them to the
>   point of desperation. And now, in
>   their desperation they've turned to
>   a man they don't fully understand.

Wayne gets up from his monitors, raises the bat-cabinet.

>   WAYNE
>   Criminals aren't complicated,
>   Alfred. We just have to figure out
>   what he's after.

>   ALFRED

Respectfully, Master Wayne, perhaps
this is a man you don't fully
understand, either.

                    ALFRED (CONT'D)
          (looks at Wayne)
I was in Burma. A long time ago.
My friends and I were working for
the local government. They were
trying to buy the loyalty of tribal
leaders, bribing them with precious
stones. But their caravans were
being raided in a forest north of
Rangoon by a bandit. We were asked
to take care of the problem, so we
started looking for the stones.
But after six months, we couldn't
find *anyone* who had traded with
him.

                    WAYNE
What were you missing?

                    ALFRED
One day I found a child playing
with a ruby as big as a tangerine.
          (shrugs)
The bandit had been throwing the
stones away.

                    WAYNE
So why was he stealing them?

                    ALFRED
Because he thought it was good
sport. Because some men aren't
looking for anything logical, like
money... they can't be bought,
bullied, reasoned or negotiated
with.
          (grave)
Some men just want to watch the
world burn.

Wayne stares at Alfred. Reaches for the bat-suit.

EXT. SKYLINE OF GOTHAM -- DAWN

MOVING over the city we hear myriad RADIO CALLS going out
over the ether. CLOSE IN on a lonely figure on top of a
skyscraper. The Batman. Listening with his million dollar
earpieces. From the babble, ONE VOICE EMERGES.

                    DISPATCH (O.S.)
          Your name, sir. Please state-

                    VOICE (O.S.)
          8th at orchard.   You'll find
          Harvey Dent there.

EXT. 8TH STREET AT ORCHARD -- DAWN

An UNMARKED and a SQUAD CAR screech to a halt. Gordon and
Ramirez get out, lead two UNIFORMS into the building.

INT. APARTMENT, EIGHT AVE. -- CONTINUOUS

The door SMASHES OPEN, Gordon- gun drawn- takes in the
scene. TWO DEAD MEN sitting at the kitchen table. They
each have a HAND OF CARDS, as if in the middle of a game.
ALL JOKERS. Gordon and Ramirez STARE at the CRUDE LEERS
carved into their faces. Their DRIVERS LICENSES are pinned
to their chests.

                    VOICE (O.S.)
          Check the names.

                    GORDON (O.S.)
             (checks licenses)
          Patrick *Harvey*. Richard *Dent*...

                    RAMIREZ
          Harvey Dent.

                    BATMAN
          I need ten minutes with the scene
          before your men contaminate it.

                    RAMIREZ
          Us contaminate it? It's because of
          you that these guys are dead in the
          first place-

                    GORDON
          Ramirez.

She stands down. Batman moves past the bodies to the wall.
Finds an embedded stray bullet. He pulls a SAWING DEVICE

from his belt- THRUSTS it into the wall and starts cutting
around the bullet.

                    GORDON (CONT'D)
             That's brick- you're gonna try and
             take ballistics off a shattered
             bullet?

                    BATMAN
             No. Fingerprints.

Ramirez looks at Gordon. Is he serious? Gordon points-

                    GORDON
             Whatever you're gonna do, do it
             fast, 'cos we know his next
             target...

Batman looks- a campaign poster: RE-ELECT MAYOR GARCIA.
The Mayor's image has a MANIC CLOWN'S GRIN and "HA,HA,HA".

INT. FOX'S OFFICE, WAYNE ENTERPRISES -- DAY

Fox is at his desk. Reese enters.

                    FOX
             What can I do for you, Mr. Reese?

                    REESE
             You asked me to do the diligence on
             the L.S.I.Holdings deal again. I
             found irregularities.

                    FOX
             Their CEO is in police custody.

                    REESE
             Not with their numbers. With
             yours. A whole division of Wayne
             Industries disappeared, overnight.
             So I went down to the archives and
             started pulling old files.

He pulls out a folded blueprint. Slides it across the
desk.

                    REESE (CONT'D)
             My kids love the Batman. I thought
             he was pretty cool, too. Out
             there, kicking some ass.

Fox picks up the piece of paper. Unfolds it. It's an old
BLUEPRINT. The image is unmistakable: **THE TUMBLER.**

                REESE (CONT'D)
      Changes things when you know it's
      just a rich kid playing dress up.

Reese points to the approval box in the corner of the page.

                REESE (CONT'D)
      Your project. Don't tell me you
      didn't recognize your baby
      pancaking cop cars on the evening
      news. Now you're getting sloppy.
      Applied Sciences was a small, dead
      department- who'd notice? But now
      you've got the *entire R and D*
      department burning cash, claiming
      it's related to *cell phones* for the
      army. What are you building him
      now? A rocket ship?

                REESE (CONT'D)
      I want ten million a year. For the
      rest of my life.

Fox looks at him. Even. Folds up the blueprint.

                FOX
      Let me get this straight. You
      think that your client, one of the
      wealthiest and most powerful men in
      the world, is secretly a vigilante
      who spends his nights beating
      criminals to a pulp with his bare
      hands...
          (deadpan)
      And now your plan is to blackmail
      this person?

Reese stares at Fox. Who smiles. And slides the blueprint
across the desk.

                FOX (CONT'D)
      Good luck.

Reese looks at it. Then at Fox. Swallows. Slides it
back.

INT. BAT-BUNKER -- DAY

Wayne hands Alfred a RIFLE BULLET scribed with a GRID. He
slots it into a clip, then loads it into a COMPUTER
CONTROLLED GATTLING GUN. He puts on ear protectors. Hits
a button.

The rifle WHIRS to life- dollying sideways, BLASTING
BULLETS into a series of identical BRICK WALL SAMPLES.

> ALFRED
> I'm not sure you made it loud
> enough, sir.

As the wall samples still smoke, Wayne steps up, carrying
the sample from the crime scene. Comparing its spread to
the new samples, he selects two and carries them to an X-
RAY SCANNER.

The machine gives the samples a 3-axis scan- HI-RES 3-D
IMAGES of the bullet fragment arrays come up on the
screen...

INT. APPLIED SCIENCES DIVISION -- DAY

The same image of the bullet fragment on a screen. Fox
hits a key and the computer 'reassembles' the bullets
according to the identifying grid on each fragment.

> FOX
> Here's your original scan...

A bullet fragment array pops on screen.

> FOX (CONT'D)
> Here's it reverse-engineered...

Fox hits a button and the unmarked bullet fragments are
reassembled. Wayne spins the roughly-shaped bullet puzzle-

> WAYNE
> And *here's* a thumb print.

Fox looks at the screen, impressed. Thinks.

> FOX
> I'll make you a copy.
> (troubled)
> Mr.Wayne, did you reassign R and D?

                         WAYNE
          Yes. Government telecommunications
          project.

                         FOX
          I wasn't aware we had any new
          government contracts. Can you-

                         WAYNE
          Lucius. I'm playing this one
          pretty close to the chest.

                         FOX
          Fair enough.

Fox looks at Wayne as he leaves. Uneasy.

INT. BAT-BUNKER -- CONTINUOUS -- INTERCUT

Wayne examines the fingerprint-

                         ALFRED
          I'll run it through all the
          databases and came up with for
          possibles.

Wayne gets up to let Alfred sit

                         WAYNE
          Cross reference the addresses...

                         WAYNE (CONT'D)
          Look for Parkside and around.

Wayne opens a HYDRAULIC DOOR, revealing a gleaming MV
AUGUSTA BRUTALE. As he moves the bike onto the lift...

                         ALFRED
          Got one. Melvin White, aggravated
          assault, moved to Arkham twice-
          1502 Randolph Apartments, just off
          State-

                         WAYNE
          Overlooking the parade.

Wayne and the bike rise on the lift.

EXT. PARKSIDE AVENUE -- DAY

The avenue has been blocked off. Onlookers line the
sidewalks. POLICE march past in dress uniform. Engel does
a stand-up on the sidewalk.

> ENGEL
> With no word from the Batman- even
> as they mourn Commissioner Loeb,
> these cops have to be wondering if
> the Joker is going to make good on
> his threat to kill the Mayor
> today...

On the buildings above, POLICE SNIPERS scan the crowd.
Gordon keys his radio-

> GORDON
> How's it looking up top?

> POLICE SNIPER
> We're tight. But frankly...
> there's a *lot* of windows up here.

Gordon looks up at the myriad buildings overlooking the
podium.

EXT. GOTHAM STREETS -- CONTINUOUS

Wayne maneuvers the Ducati through the traffic. He pulls
up near a parade barricade- dismounts and slips into an
alley.

INT. TENEMENT -- CONTINUOUS

Some of the building's hard-luck TENANTS eye Wayne as he
counts doors down the hallway. He finds 1502...

EXT. PARKSIDE AVENUE -- LATER

A SEA OF POLICE fills the Avenue. In the center, three
grieving families and an HONOR GUARD. The Mayor at the
podium. Gordon behind. Dent is seated with Rachel.

> THE MAYOR
> ...and as we recognize the
> sacrifice of these officers, we
> must remember that vigilance is the
> price of safety.

INT. TENEMENT -- CONTINUOUS

Wayne enters: EIGHT MEN IN UNDERSHIRTS, bound, gagged,
blindfolded. A SNIPER SCOPE on a tripod at the window.
Wayne moves to the first man, RIPS the tape from his mouth.

> MAN
> (breathing hard)
> Took... they took our guns, our
> uniforms...

EXT. PARKSIDE AVENUE -- CONTINUOUS

Gordon scans the crowd. The Mayor wraps up- the Honor
Guard steps forward, raises weapons...

EXT. ROOFTOP OVERLOOKING PARKSIDE -- CONTINUOUS

A POLICE SNIPER scans the windows of the tenement...

INT. TENEMENT -- CONTINUOUS

Wayne RACES to the window, looks through the SCOPE to see:

EXT. STATE STREET -- CONTINUOUS

THE HONOR GUARD TURN THEIR WEAPONS ON THE MAYOR. One
SMILES, flesh-colored makeup over his scars. THE JOKER.

Gordon LEAPS FORWARD- they FIRE- GORDON TAKES SHOTS TO THE
BACK as he SLAMS the Mayor to the ground-

EXT. ROOFTOP OVERLOOKING PARKSIDE -- CONTINUOUS

The Police Sniper SPOTS Wayne at the window- SHOOTS-

INT. TENEMENT -- CONTINUOUS

Wayne DUCKS as SHOTS erupt around the window-

EXT. PARKSIDE -- CONTINUOUS

PANDEMONIUM erupts-One of the honor guard is TAGGED IN THE
LEG- GOES DOWN. The others MELT into the CHAOS.

On the podium, Stephens rolls Gordon over... he is not
moving.

EXT. SIDE STREET OFF PARKSIDE -- MOMENTS LATER

CHAOS. Dent approaches an ambulance sitting in the alley. Two cops jump out and run over to their commander. Dent steps up into the back.

INT. AMBULANCE -- CONTINUOUS

The Joker's thug sits there. Handcuffed. A PARAMEDIC bandages his leg. Cops run past, barking orders.

> DENT
> Tell me what you know about the
> Joker.

The Joker's thug looks at Dent. Smirks. Dent looks down. Exasperated. Looks back up at the Joker's Thug. Spots something- moves closer- the man's uniform... his name tag...

OFFICER RACHEL DAWES.

Dent, breathing hard, looks around: the paramedic jumps out, rushing to help a FALLEN OFFICER. Dent spies the keys in the ignition. Jumps into the driver's seat...

EXT. GORDON'S HOUSE -- DUSK

Barbara Gordon stands in the doorway, scared. Stephens and a UNIFORMED OFFICER stand in front of her.

> STEPHENS
> I'm sorry, Barbara.

James Gordon pushes past his mother to look at Stephens. Barbara tries to push him back inside.

> BARBARA
> Jimmy, go play with your sister...

James stays just inside the door.

> STEPHENS
> I'm sorry.

Barbara stares at Stephens. Then looks past him.

> BARBARA
> Are you out there?! Are you?!

James spots something- Batman, perched in the shadows.

                         BARBARA (CONT'D)
              You brought this on us! This
              craziness! *You* did! You brought
              this...!

She collapses into Stephens's arms. Batman hangs his head.

EXT. ROOF, MCU -- NIGHT

Detectives from MCU stand around the lit bat-signal.

                         STEPHENS
              Switch it off- he ain't coming.

                         STEPHENS
              He doesn't want to talk to us. God
              help whoever he *does* want to talk
              to-

INT. NIGHTCLUB -- NIGHT

Strobe lights. Pounding music. Maroni is in a booth at
the side with his MISTRESS. His bodyguards are around the
table.

                         MISTRESS
                    (shouting over
                     music)
              Can't we go someplace quieter! We
              can't hear each other talk!

                         MARONI
              I don't wanna hear you talk.

                         MISTRESS
                    (can't hear)
              What?!

One of Maroni's Bodyguards DROPS- Maroni looks over- in the
strobe lights- Batman SAVAGES his bodyguards- people RUN,
TERRIFIED. Maroni starts to get out of his seat- Batman
LANDS like a panther on the table in front of him-

INT. MCU -- NIGHT

Rachel moves through the chaotic bullpen at MCU-
EYEWITNESSES, civilian and cop are being questioned.
Rachel's phone rings.

                         RACHEL

                    Harvey, where are you?!

          INTERCUT with Dent in an INDISTINCT interior setting.

                              DENT
                         Where are you?

                              RACHEL
                         Where *you* should be- at Major
                         Crimes trying to sort through all
                         the-

                              DENT
                         Rachel, listen to me. You're not
                         safe there.

                              RACHEL
                         This is Gordon's unit, Harvey-

                              DENT
                         Gordon's gone, Rachel.

                              RACHEL
                         He vouched for these men-

                              DENT
                         And he's gone. The Joker's named
                         you next.

          Rachel looks around the bullpen. Eyeing the detectives.

                              DENT (CONT'D)
                         Rachel, I can't let anything happen
                         to you. I love you too much.

                              DENT
                         Is there someone, *anyone* in this
                         city we can trust?

                              RACHEL
                         Bruce. We can trust Bruce Wayne.

                              DENT
                         Rachel, I know he's your friend
                         but-

                              RACHEL
                         Trust me, Harvey, Bruce's penthouse
                         is now the safest place in the
                         city.

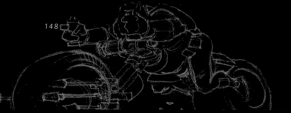

                    DENT
          Okay. Go straight there. Don't
          tell anyone where you're going.
          I'll find you there.

Wider shows us we are-

INT. BASEMENT, CONDEMNED BUILDING -- CONTINUOUS

                    DENT
          I love you.

Dent hangs up the phone. TAPED to a chair in front of
Dent- the Joker's Thug, blindfolded. Dent RIPS off the
blindfold...

EXT. FIRE ESCAPE -- NIGHT

Maroni opens his eyes. Batman is holding him by the
collar.

                    BATMAN
          I want the Joker.

                    MARONI
             (looks down)
          From one professional to another-if
          you're trying to scare someone,
          pick a better spot. From this
          height the fall wouldn't kill me.

                    BATMAN
          I'm counting on it.

Batman lets go. Maroni FALLS. And SCREAMS.

EXT. SIDEWALK -- NIGHT

Maroni NAILS the pavement. CLUTCHES at his leg, which is
badly broken. Batman FLIES down, landing over him- hauls
him up. Maroni HOLLERS in pain.

                    BATMAN
          Where is he?

                    MARONI
          I don't know, *he* found us-

                    BATMAN
          He must have friends.

                    MARONI
          Friends? You met this guy?

                    BATMAN
          Someone knows where he is.

Maroni looks up at Batman. Sneering.

                    MARONI
          No one's gonna tell you anything-
          they're wise to your act- you got
          rules... the Joker, he's got no
          rules. No one's gonna cross him
          for you. You want this guy, you
          got one way. And you already know
          what that is. Just take off that
          mask and let him come find you.

Batman DROPS Maroni.

                    MARONI (CONT'D)
          Or you want to let a couple more
          people get killed while you make up
          your mind?

INT. BASEMENT, CONDEMNED BUILDING -- NIGHT

Dent shows the Joker's Thug a GUN. Bullets. Loads the
gun. SHOVES it in his face-

                    DENT
          You wanna play games?

Dent PUSHES the gun against the thug's head with REAL
MALICE. Pulls it away and FIRES. The Thug FLINCHES. Dent
puts the gun barrel against the thug's temple-

                    JOKER'S THUG
               (rattled)
          You wouldn't...

And pulls his lucky coin out of his pocket.

                    DENT
          No. I wouldn't. That's why I'm
          not going to leave it up to *me*.
               (shows him coin)
          Heads- you get to *keep* your head.
          Tails... not so lucky. So, you
          want to tell me about the Joker?

The Thug, scared, says nothing. Dent FLICKS the coin into
the air. SLAPS it onto the back of his gun hand (aiming
with wrist horizontal). Dent shows him the coin. Heads.
The Thug exhales, SHAKING.

                    DENT (CONT'D)
          Go again?

                    JOKER'S THUG
               (sobbing)
          I don't *know* anything!

                    DENT
          You're not playing the odds,
          friend.

Dent tosses the coin again. This time IT DOESN'T LAND.
Dent looks up. Batman is there.

                    BATMAN
          You'd leave a man's life to chance?

                    DENT
          Not exactly.

                    BATMAN
          His name's Schiff, Thomas. He's a
          paranoid schizophrenic, a former
          patient at Arkham. The kind of
          mind the Joker attracts.

Batman moves away from Schiff.

                    BATMAN (CONT'D)
          What do expect to learn from him?

Dent is shivering with frustration.

                    DENT
          The Joker killed Gordon- and, and
          Loeb. He's going to kill *Rachel*...

                    BATMAN
          You're the symbol of hope that I
          could never be. Your stand against
          organized crime is the first
          legitimate ray of light in Gotham
          for *decades*. If anyone saw this,
          everything would be undone- all the
          criminals you got off the streets

would be released. And Jim Gordon
will have died for nothing.

Batman hands Dent his lucky coin.

                    BATMAN (CONT'D)
          You're going to call a press
          conference. Tomorrow morning.

                    DENT
          Why?

                    BATMAN
          No one else will die because of me.
          Gotham is in *your* hands, now.

                    DENT
          You can't! You can't give in!

But Batman is gone.

INT. BEDROOM, WAYNE PENTHOUSE -- NIGHT

Rachel watches Gotham through the window. Wayne enters.

                    RACHEL
          Harvey called. He says Batman is
          going to turn himself in.

                    WAYNE
          I have no choice.

                    RACHEL
          You honestly think it's going to
          stop the Joker from killing?

                    WAYNE
          Perhaps not. But I've got enough
          blood on my hands. I've seen, now,
          what I would have to become to stop
          men like him.

Rachel looks at Wayne. She cannot help him.

                    WAYNE (CONT'D)
          You once told me that if the day
          came when I was *finished*...

Wayne moves towards her.

                    WAYNE (CONT'D)
          We'd be together.

                    RACHEL
          Bruce, don't make me your one hope
          for a normal life-

Wayne takes her in his arms.

                    WAYNE
          But did you mean it?

                    RACHEL
          Yes.

They kiss. Then separate. She looks sadly into his eyes.

                    RACHEL (CONT'D)
          But they won't let us be together
          after you turn yourself in.

Wayne nods. Leaves. She watches him go.

INT. BAT-BUNKER -- DAWN

Alfred shovels DOCUMENTS into an incinerator- blueprints,
designs, files. He pauses, looking down at a book.

                    ALFRED
          Even the logs?

                    WAYNE
          Anything that could lead back to
          Lucius or Rachel.

Alfred tosses the book onto the fire. STARES at Wayne.

                    WAYNE (CONT'D)
          People are dying, Alfred. What
          would you have me do?

Alfred looks into Wayne's eyes with a fearsome gaze.

                    ALFRED
          Endure, Master Wayne. Take it.
          They'll hate you for it, but that's
          the point of Batman... he can be
          the outcast. He can make the
          choice no one else can face. The
          right choice.

Wayne shakes his head.

> WAYNE
> Today I've found out what Batman
> can't do. He can't endure *this*.

> WAYNE
>   (rueful smile)
> Today you get to say 'I told you
> so'.

> ALFRED
> Today, I don't want to.
>   (beat)
> Although I did bloody tell you.

Wayne sinks the Bat-suit, Alfred closes the incinerator.
They head for the lift.

> ALFRED (CONT'D)
> I suppose they'll lock me up as
> well. Your accomplice.

> WAYNE
> Accomplice? I'm going to tell them
> the whole thing was your idea.

They power down, leaving the Bat-bunker in darkness.

OMITTED

INT. PRESS ROOM, SUPERIOR COURT -- DAY

A capacity crowd of REPORTERS, COPS, and PUBLIC. Dent is
at the podium. Wayne sits in the crowd.

> DENT
> Ladies and Gentlemen, thank you for
> coming. I've called this press
> conference for two reasons.
> Firstly, to assure the citizens of
> Gotham that everything that can be
> done over the Joker killing is
> being done. Secondly, because the
> Batman has offered to turn himself
> in-

The crowd REACTS-

> HECKLER

So where is he?!

                    DENT
     But first. Let's consider the
     situation: should we give in to
     this terrorist's demands? Do we
     really think that—

                    REPORTER
     You'd rather protect an outlaw
     vigilante than the lives of
     citizens?!

The crowd noisily assents. Dent calmly motions quiet.

                    DENT
     The Batman *is* an outlaw...

INT. WAYNE PENTHOUSE -- CONTINUOUS

Rachel is watching the press conference on TV.

                    DENT (O.S.)
     But that's not why we're demanding
     he turn himself in. We're doing it
     because we're **scared.** *We've been*
     happy to let Batman clean up our
     streets for us until now—

INT. PRESS ROOM, SUPERIOR COURT -- CONTINUOUS

                    HECKLER
     Things are worse than ever!

Wayne looks at the Heckler. At the angry crowd. Dent
leans over the podium. Impassioned.

                    DENT
     Yes. They are. But *the night is*
     darkest just before the dawn. And
     I promise you, the dawn *is* coming.
          (the crowd quiets)
     One day, the Batman will have to
     answer for the laws he's broken—
     but to **us**, not to this madman.

The crowd seems moved by his words, then, a CHANT—

                    COP HECKLER
     NO MORE DEAD COPS!!

Appreciative noise.

                    REPORTER
          WHERE *IS* THE BATMAN?

People take up the chant. Dent has lost them. He knows
it.

                    DENT
          So be it.
               (turns to officers)
          Take the Batman into custody.

At this, a HUSH DESCENDS. Wayne is sitting towards the
back. Hungry eyes scan the room. Wayne starts to rise...
DENT OFFERS HIS OWN WRISTS TO THE OFFICERS-

                    DENT (CONT'D)
          I am the Batman.

A beat. Wayne stares.

INT. WAYNE PENTHOUSE -- CONTINUOUS

Rachel STARES as Dent is arrested on TV. Appalled.

INT. WAYNE PENTHOUSE -- DAY

Rachel comes up to Alfred. Upset.

                    RACHEL
          Why is he letting Harvey do this,
          Alfred?

                    ALFRED
          I don't know. He went down to the
          press conference-

                    RACHEL
          And just stood by?!

                    ALFRED
          Perhaps both Bruce and Mr.Dent
          believe that Batman stands for
          something more important than a
          terrorist's whims, Miss Dawes, even
          if *everyone* hates him for it.
          That's the sacrifice he's making-
          to not be a hero. To be something
          more.

                    RACHEL
          Well, you're right about one thing-
          letting Harvey take the fall is not
          heroic.

Rachel holds out an ENVELOPE.

                    RACHEL (CONT'D)
          You know Bruce best, Alfred...
          give it to him when the time is
          right.

                    ALFRED
          How will I know?

                    RACHEL
          It's not sealed.

Alfred takes the envelope. Rachel gives him a kiss.

                    RACHEL (CONT'D)
          Goodbye, Alfred.

                    ALFRED
          Goodbye, Rachel.

INT. CELL, MCU -- EVENING

A Detective unlocks the cell and lets Rachel inside.

                    DENT
          I'm sorry, I didn't have time to
          talk this through with you.

                    RACHEL
          Don't offer yourself as bait,
          Harvey.

                    DENT
          They're transferring me to central
          holding. This is the Joker's
          chance, and when he attacks, Batman
          will take him down.

                    RACHEL
          No. This is too dangerous-

The Detective knocks. Dent rises.

EXT. COURTYARD MCU -- EVENING

Detectives stare at Dent as he is led, shackled, to the waiting CONVOY. Stephens begins CLAPPING- a handful join in, but most remain silent. Rachel follows him to the back of an armored vehicle.

                    RACHEL
          He's using you as bait- but he
          doesn't know if he can get the
          Joker- he's failed so far.

                    DENT
          How do you know what he's thinking?

                    RACHEL
               (beat)
          I just do, okay? Harvey, this
          isn't just about you, what about
          all the people counting on you to
          turn this city around? Tell
          everyone the truth-

Dent kisses her. Pulls out his LUCKY COIN-

                    DENT
          Heads I go through with it.

                    RACHEL
          This is your *life*... you don't
          leave something like this to
          chance...

Dent tosses it at her- Rachel catches it. Looks. Heads.

                    DENT
               (sincere)
          I'm not.

She turns it over: IT IS DOUBLE-HEADED. She looks up- the DOORS CLOSE on his smile. She shakes her head. Torn.

                    RACHEL
          You make your own luck.

As SWATS file into the back of the support vehicles-

                    ACTING COMISSIONER
          We get this guy to County and he's
          their problem. The streets along
          your route will be cleared. The
          convoy stops FOR NO REASON...

INT. ARMORED CAR -- CONTINUOUS

A Swat with a shotgun climbs into the cab. Pulls on his
mask. Looks over at the DRIVER, who's already wearing his.

                    SHOTGUN SWAT
          Hope you've got some moves.

EXT. TENTH AVENUE, DOWNTOWN -- CONTINUOUS

The convoy ROCKETS past a roadblock.

INT. ARMORED CAR -- CONTINUOUS

The Swats are staring at Dent, fascinated. He smiles.

EXT. INTERSECTION -- CONTINUOUS

An Officer holding up traffic. A TRUCK pulls up.

                    OFFICER
          You wait like everybody else, pal.

A SHOTGUN BLAST sends the Officer flying. A second blast
illuminates the shooter's face: the Joker.

INT. LEAD PATROL CAR, CONVOY -- CONTINUOUS

The SWAT behind the wheel of the lead black-and-white slows
as he sees something burning in the intersection ahead.

EXT. AVENUE -- CONTINUOUS

Overhead, a police HELICOPTER checks the route, hovering
above a burning FIRE TRUCK, BLOCKING the road.

INT. ARMORED CAR -- CONTINUOUS

The Driver is all business. The radio CRACKLES.

                    RADIO
          All units, be advised. All units
          will exit down Cheviot west and
          proceed north on lower 5th avenue.

                    SHOTGUN SWAT
          Lower 5th? We'll be like ducks in
          a barrel down there.

EXT. SURFACE STREETS -- CONTINUOUS

The convoy disappears down the exit ramp.

EXT. LOWER FIFTH AVENUE -- NIGHT

The convoy rolls through the subterranean streets. A GARBAGE TRUCK pulls up behind and casually SWIPES the rear vehicles of the convoy off the road...

INT. ARMORED CAR -- CONTINUOUS

                    SHOTGUN SWAT
          Get us out of here!

The Driver NAILS the gas-

EXT. LOWER FIFTH -- CONTINUOUS

The Garbage Truck pushes hard on the armored car, ramming its rear bumper, FORCING it forward.

OMITTED

INT. ARMORED CAR -- NIGHT

The Driver watches the Truck fill his rear view. Shotgun Swat picks up the radio.

                    SHOTGUN SWAT
          We've got company back here-

EXT. LOWER FIFTH AVENUE -- NIGHT

A SECOND TRUCK SMASHES into the SWAT van at the head of the convoy, SMASHING it through the concrete barriers and INTO THE RIVER. The truck is branded "LAUGHTER" but and "S" has been spayed at the front to make "SLAUGHTER" with "HA, HA, HA" all over the side...

The Joker's Truck DODGES between the support columns and into the oncoming lane- pulls alongside the armored car.

The Driver looks over. The cargo door on the truck slides open. Inside, the Joker, holding a machine gun.

The armored car LOCKS up its brakes, but the garbage truck pushes it forward as the Joker fires- BULLETS slamming into the side of the vehicle-

INT. REAR CABIN, ARMORED CAR -- CONTINUOUS

Dent is calm as the SWATS FLINCH from the bullet
indentations-

INT. UP FRONT, ARMORED CAR -- CONTINUOUS

Shotgun SWAT STARES at the Joker.

INT. REAR TRAILER OF TRUCK -- NIGHT

The Joker drops his machine gun and picks up and RPG. He
stops- SEES something up ahead, racing towards the second
truck- the BATMOBILE. The Joker stares, fascinated, as-

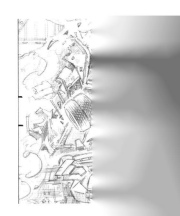

EXT. LOWER FIFTH -- CONTINUOUS

-THE BATMOBILE PLOWS STRAIGHT INTO THE SECOND TRUCK- the
low-profile car sending the truck UP INTO THE CONCRETE
CEILING- the Batmobile carries on through, as the TRUCK
DISINTEGRATES.

INT. TRUCK -- NIGHT

The Joker looks back to the batmobile, amused.

                    JOKER'S THUG
          Is that him-?

                    THE JOKER
          Anyone could be driving that thing-
          stay on Dent.

The Joker lines up his RPG and prepares to fire-

INT. ARMORED CAR -- CONTINUOUS

Shotgun SWAT's eyes go wide at the Joker's weapon- the
Driver JAMS the brakes-

OMITTED

EXT. LOWER FIFTH -- CONTINUOUS

The Armored Car CRASHES BACK against the Garbage Truck,
BRAKING, SCRAPING, SLOWING just enough- the RPG SLAMS into
the SQUAD CAR in front of them and EXPLODES- the armored
car BURSTS through the fireball and continues.

OMITTED

EXT. LOWER FIFTH -- CONTINUOUS

The Batmobile SPINS around to rejoin the pursuit.

INT. JOKER'S TRUCK -- NIGHT

The Joker turns his men to RELOAD his RPG-

>   THE JOKER
>   Do me up-

Turns back- levels his RPG out the window. Aims.

INT. BATMOBILE -- NIGHT

Batman watches as the Joker prepares to fire. Several rows
of cars separate them. He toggles the afterburner.

INT. PASSENGER CAR -- NIGHT

Two small children in the back of the car watch as the
Batmobile ROCKETS overhead.

EXT. LOWER LEVEL STREET -- NIGHT

The Joker steadies the RPG and FIRES- the Batmobile CRASHES
down into the open space between the two vehicles- taking
the hit from the RPG which EXPLODES-

The rear of the Batmobile EXPLODES- SPINNING the FLAMING
car-

INT. ARMORED CAR -- NIGHT

SWATS react to the EXPLOSION. Dent is calm.

INT. CAB OF JOKER'S TRUCK -- CONTINUOUS

The Driver takes a DEBRIS HIT to the head-

INT. TRUCK -- CONTINUOUS

The Joker CACKLES with delight as he is THROWN AROUND the
rear of the trailer-

INT. BATMOBILE -- CONTINUOUS

Batman WRESTLES the pod controls, SPINNING on the GYRO-

EXT. LOWER LEVEL STREET -- CONTINUOUS

The Batmobile flips over to come to rest in a smoking heap-
the front end intact, rear wheels scattered across the
roadway. A small crowd gathers.

OMITTED

EXT. LOWER LEVEL STREET -- CONTINUOUS

The Joker JUMPS down from the truck, still giggling like a
kid- looks back at the Batmobile's destruction-

                        THE JOKER
              Whoever he was... he ain't now.

The Joker YANKS his dead driver out of the cab, JUMPS over
him to take the wheel and pull back onto the roadway.

EXT. LOWER LEVEL STREET -- CONTINUOUS

The armored car pulls ahead, the Joker's truck in hot
pursuit.

INT. ARMORED CAR -- CONTINUOUS

Shotgun SWAT glances in the rear view mirror, slaps the
dash-

                        SHOTGUN SWAT
              Let's get topside- we need that air
              support!

EXT. LOWER LEVEL STREET -- CONTINUOUS

The armored car PULLS onto a RAMP, heading up. The Joker's
Truck follows.

EXT. LOWER LEVEL STREET -- CONTINUOUS

People stare at the smoking wreck, inching closer...

INT. BATMOBILE -- CONTINUOUS

Batman adjusts his position. Hits a button-

                        BATMOBILE VOICE
              Damage catastrophic. Initiate
              eject and self-destruct.

Arm guards GRAB Batman's forearms as EXPLOSIVE BOLTS FIRE
all around the pod...

BATMOBILE VOICE (O.S.) (CONT'D)
Goodbye.

EXT. LOWER LEVEL STREET -- CONTINUOUS

The crowd JUMPS- PANELS of the front of the car BLOW OUT-

The crowd stares, OPEN-MOUTHED, as Batman EMERGES, HOISTED
UP AND OUT of the flaming car by the FRONT POD- LEVERING
OVER the FRONT WHEEL... the pod PUSHES the OTHER WHEEL IN
FRONT to form a type of MOTORCYCLE-

The BAT-POD SHOOTS FORWARD, bursting free as the Batmobile
DETONATES, DYING in a MASSIVE FIREBALL... Batman's cape
SUCKS TOGETHER, forming a TIGHT PACK on his shoulders,
clear of the CHURNING REAR TIRE of the bat-pod...

EXT. PARKSIDE -- CONTINUOUS

The armored car races down the street- the CHOPPER dips
low.

PILOT (O.S.)
We're back on point- and ready to
give some of their own medicine-

INT. POLICE CHOPPER -- CONTINUOUS

A Cop pulls out an ASSAULT RIFLE. COCKS it-

INT. CAB OF JOKER'S TRUCK -- CONTINUOUS

The Joker FIGHTS with the truck's gearbox, turns to his
Thug-

THE JOKER
Tee 'em up.

The Thug GRABS his radio.

EXT. FIRE ESCAPE -- CONTINUOUS

A Joker Thug in clown mask loads up the cable gun seen in
the bank heist.

EXT. SECOND FIRE ESCAPE -- CONTINUOUS

Another thug loads his own cable gun...

INT. PASSENGER CAR, LOWER LEVEL STREET -- NIGHT

A motorist stares through his rear-view mirror, transfixed, as the bat-pod TEARS past. He YELPS as the bat-pod SMASHES the wing mirror from his car.

EXT. LOWER LEVEL STREET -- NIGHT

Batman accelerates, oblivious to the STACCATO of CLEAVED wing mirrors as the bat-pod RAZORS through traffic- CROSSES a BUSY INTERSECTION- The bat-pod CUTS off the crowded lower level street, ROARING over into the PARKING LANES-

Batman squeezes his triggers- BLASTING at PARKED CARS, BLOWING them out of the way, literally CANNONING A PATH for the pod...

OMITTED

EXT. TRAIN STATION -- CONTINUOUS

The Bat-Pod CANNONS through the glass doors and RACES through the station/mall- COMMUTERS screaming and diving out of the way-

The Bat-Pod races up the stairs and onto the upper street-

EXT. PARKSIDE -- CONTINUOUS

The Joker's Thugs FIRE THE CABLES ACROSS THE STREET AT SEVENTH FLOOR LEVEL... they pull TAUT as the Chopper approaches, unawares... the Chopper CATCHES on the cables, GOING DOWN in a FIERY BALL that BARRELS along the street towards the armored car...

INT. ARMORED CAR -- CONTINUOUS

The Driver steers around the flaming wreckage as the Shotgun SWAT SHUTS HIS EYES-

EXT. NARROW ALLEY -- CONTINUOUS

The Bat-pod TEARS down a narrow alley blocked with DUMPSTERS- CANNONS the dumpsters to make a path-

INT. OMITTED

INT. CAB OF JOKER'S TRUCK -- NIGHT

The Joker hands the wheel to his man- takes a submachine gun-

                              THUG
          Boss?

The Joker looks ahead to see the Bat-pod emerge from the
alley in a cloud of fire, SKIDDING SIDEWAYS IMPOSSIBLY- it
RACES TOWARDS THEM-

                           THE JOKER
          Guess it *was* him.

EXT. PARKSIDE -- NIGHT

The Bat-pod RACES straight at the Joker's truck- FIRES A
HARPOON at the Joker's truck- it IMPACTS low, below the
bumper-

INT. TRUCK -- CONTINUOUS

The Joker's Thug DUCKS, then comes back up, beaming.

                        JOKER'S THUG
          He missed!

EXT. PARKSIDE -- CONTINUOUS

Batman SWERVES past the Joker's truck, SLALOMS, wrapping
the CABLES around a LAMP POST, SPINNING to a halt to
watch...

EXT. PARKSIDE -- CONTINUOUS

The cable goes TAUT, RIPPING one post from its foundation-
the TRUCK'S FRONT WHEELS CATCH, FLIPPING IT END OVER END...

The Joker crawls from the wreckage. He jumps over the
median and starts waving his pistol at oncoming traffic.
Batman GUNS the bat-pod and rides it up and over the
median.

INT. ARMORED CAR -- NIGHT

The Driver slows the car, pulls to the side.

                        SHOTGUN SWAT
          What the hell are you doing?

EXT. PARKSIDE -- NIGHT

The Joker walks towards the Bat-pod, which SPEEDS towards him. He is FIRING his gun RANDOMLY at the oncoming traffic.

> THE JOKER
> Hit me. Come on. *Hit me.*

Batman watches as the Joker holds out his arms. Waiting for impact. There is no room to go around him.

Batman LOCKS UP THE BRAKES.

The Joker watches as Batman DUMPS the bike, rather than smashing into him. Batman SLAMS into the wall.

The Joker's thug reach Batman first. He is unconscious. The first Thug pulls at the mask. An ELECTRIC SHOCK from the bat-suit THROWS him back. The Joker LAUGHS. Flicks his switchblade. Crouches-

> VOICE (O.S.)
> Drop it.

> THE JOKER
> Just give me a second.

The gun is COCKED. The Joker drops the knife. Sits. Looks back. Behind them is the armored car. The man standing over him is the Driver. He pulls off his helmet.

It's JIM GORDON. Back from the dead.

> GORDON
> We got you, you son of a bitch.

INT. ARMORED CAR -- MOMENTS LATER

Dent looks up as the door swings open to reveal Gordon. Dent GRINS.

> DENT
> *Lieutenant*, you *do* like to play it
> pretty close to the chest...

> GORDON
> We got him, Harvey.

Dent nods. Respect in his eyes. They shake hands.

EXT. PARKSIDE -- NIGHT

167

A small army of cops have sealed off the roadway. Gordon
pulls away in the squad car containing the Joker.

REPORTERS clamor for an interview with Dent, who is being
helped out of the van by the SWATS. Ramirez pushes through
the pack, shoving reporters aside.

                    RAMIREZ
          Let him be! He's been through
          enough-

Dent follows Ramirez to a squad car- Wuertz is in the
driver's seat. Dent smiles at Ramirez as she opens the
rear door.

                    DENT
          Thanks, detective- I've got a date
          with a pretty upset fiancÈe.

                    RAMIREZ
          I figured, counselor.

Ramirez shuts the door on Dent. Signals Wuertz to pull
out.

INT. HOLDING, MCU, GOTHAM CENTRAL -- NIGHT

The Joker sits in a holding cage. His makeup has run, his
clothes a mess- but his calm lends him an odd dignity.
COPS SMASH their night sticks against the bars near the
Joker's head. The Joker does not flinch.

                    GORDON
          Stand away! All of you. I don't
          want *anything* for his mob lawyer to
          use, understand? Handle this guy
          like he's made of glass.

The Mayor walks in. Shakes Gordon's hand.

                    MAYOR
          Back from the dead.

                    GORDON
          I couldn't chance my family's
          safety.

The Mayor looks over at the Joker in his cage.

                    MAYOR

What do we got?

> GORDON
> *Nothing*. No matches on prints,
> DNA, dental. Clothing is custom,
> no labels. Nothing in his pockets
> but knives and lint. No name, no
> other alias... nothing.

> MAYOR
> Go home, Gordon. The clown'll keep
> till morning. Get some rest-
> you're going to need it. Tomorrow,
> you take the big job.
>   (off look)
> You don't have any say in the
> matter.
>   (louder, for all)
> *Commissioner* Gordon.

The cops in M.C.U. start CHEERING.

EXT. GORDON HOME -- NIGHT

Gordon rings the bell. Barbara answers it, dressed in
black.

> GORDON
> I couldn't tell you. I couldn't
> risk-

She SLAPS Gordon. He grabs her, holds her tight as she
sobs.

INT. HOLDING, MCU, GOTHAM CENTRAL -- NIGHT

The Joker's men are processed. In the harsh light, the men
look a little ridiculous in their clown make-up. DETECTIVE
MURPHY turns to Stephens.

> DETECTIVE
> Look at these ugly bastards.

One of the men, walks over, clutching at his belly.

> FAT THUG
> I don't feel good.

> DETECTIVE MURPHY

You're a cop killer. You're lucky
to be feeling anything below the
neck.

Alone in his cage, the Joker smiles at this.

INT. KIDS' BEDROOM, GORDON HOME -- NIGHT

Gordon crouches by his son's beside. He reaches out to
touch James Jr's cheek. James's eyes open. Staring at his
dad as if still dreaming.

                    JAMES
               (whispers)
          Did Batman save you, dad?

Gordon looks at his son. A little pride seeps in.

                    GORDON
          Actually, this time *I* saved *him*.

Gordon's phone rings-

INT. MAJOR CRIMES UNIT, GOTHAM CENTRAL -- NIGHT

Gordon PUSHES through the swarm of detectives crowded into
the observation room. The Joker can be seen through the
glass, as well as on a large MONITOR. Sitting there.
Calm.

                    GORDON
          Has he said anything, yet?

Ramirez shakes her head. Gordon PUSHES through a door...

INT. INTERROGATION, MCU, GOTHAM CENTRAL -- NIGHT

The Joker, in near darkness. Gordon walks in. Sits.

                    THE JOKER
          Evening, Commissioner.

                    GORDON
          Harvey Dent never made it home.

                    THE JOKER
          Of course not.

                    GORDON
          What have you done with him?

                         THE JOKER
                    (laughs)
               Me? I was right here. Who did you
               leave him with? Your people?
               Assuming, of course, that they are
               your people not Maroni's...
                    (off look)
               Does it depress you, Lieutenant, to
               know how alone you are?

Gordon can't help glancing at the mounted CAMERA.

                         THE JOKER (CONT'D)
               Does it make you feel *responsible*
               for Harvey Dent's current
               predicament?

                         GORDON
               Where is he?

                         THE JOKER
               What time is it?

                         GORDON
               What difference does that make?

                         THE JOKER
               Depending on the time, he might be
               in one spot.
                    (smiles)
               Or *several.*

Gordon stands. Moves to the Joker. Undoes his handcuffs.

                         GORDON
               If we're going to play games, I'm
               going to need a cup of coffee.

                         THE JOKER
               The good cop, bad cop routine?

Gordon pauses, hand on the doorknob.

                         GORDON
               Not exactly.

Gordon steps out. The overhead lights COME ON. BATMAN IS
BEHIND HIM. The Joker BLINKS in the HARSH WHITE LIGHT.

WHAM! The Joker's face HITS the table- comes up for air-
CRACK! CRACK! To the head. Batman is in front of him.
The Joker stares, fascinated. Bleeding.

>   THE JOKER
>   Never start with the head... victim
>   gets fuzzy. Can't feel the next-

CRACK! Batman's fist SMACKS down on the Joker's fingers.

>   THE JOKER (CONT'D)
>   (calm)
>   See?

>   BATMAN
>   You wanted me. Here I am.

>   THE JOKER
>   I wanted to see what you'd *do*. And
>   you didn't disappoint...
>   (laughs)
>   You let five people *die*. Then you
>   let Dent take your place. Even to
>   a guy like me... that's *cold*-

>   BATMAN
>   Where's Dent?

>   THE JOKER
>   Those mob fools want you gone so
>   they can get back to the way things
>   were. But I know the truth-
>   there's no going back. You've
>   changed things. Forever.

>   BATMAN
>   Then why do you want to kill me?

The Joker starts LAUGHING. After a moment he's laughing so
hard it sounds like SOBBING.

>   THE JOKER
>   Kill you? I don't want to kill
>   you. What would I do without you?
>   Go back to ripping off Mob dealers?
>   No *you*...
>   (points)
>   You. Complete. Me.

                    BATMAN
          You're garbage who kills for money.

                    THE JOKER
          Don't talk like one of them- you're
          not, even if you'd like to be. To
          them you're a freak like me... they
          just *need* you right now.

He regards Batman with something approaching pity.

                    THE JOKER (CONT'D)
          But as soon as they don't, they'll
          cast you out like a leper.

The Joker looks into Batman's eyes. Searching.

                    THE JOKER (CONT'D)
          Their morals, their code... it's a
          bad joke. Dropped at the first
          sign of trouble. They're only as
          good as the world *allows* them to
          be. You'll see- I'll show you...
          when the chips are down, these
          civilized people... they'll *eat
          each other*.
                    (grins)
          See, I'm not a monster... I'm just
          ahead of the curve.

Batman GRABS the Joker and pulls him upright.

INT. OBSERVATION ROOM, MCU, GOTHAM CENTRAL -- NIGHT

One of the Detectives moves for the door. Gordon stops
him.

                    GORDON
          He's in control.

INT. INTERROGATION ROOM, MCU, GOTHAM CENTRAL -- NIGHT

Batman HOISTS the Joker up by the neck.

                    BATMAN
          Where's Dent?

                    THE JOKER
          You have these rules. And you
          think they'll save you.

                    BATMAN
          I have one rule.

                    THE JOKER
          Then that's the one you'll have to
          break. To know the truth.

                    BATMAN
          Which is?

                    THE JOKER
               (smiles)
          The only sensible way to live in
          this world is *without* rules.
          Tonight you're going to break your
          one rule...

Batman leans in to the Joker.

                    BATMAN
          I'm considering it.

                    THE JOKER
          There are just minutes left- so,
          you'll *have* to play my little game
          if you want to save...
               (with relish)
          ...one of them.

                    BATMAN
          Them?

                    THE JOKER
          For a while I thought you really
          were Dent, the way you threw
          yourself after her-

Batman DROPS the Joker- RIPS up a bolted-down chair-

INT. OBSERVATION ROOM, MCU, GOTHAM CENTRAL -- NIGHT

Gordon MOVES for the door-

INT. OBSERVATION ROOM, MCU -- CONTINUOUS

Batman JAMS the chair under the doorknob- PICKS up the
Joker and HURLS him into the two-way glass. The glass
SPIDERS.

INT. INTERROGATION ROOM, MCU, GOTHAM CENTRAL -- NIGHT

The Joker, bleeding from nose and mouth, LAUGHS at Batman.

>   THE JOKER
>   Look at you *go*... does Harvey *know*
>   about you and his-?

The Joker SMASHES into the wall- SLIDES to the floor.
Batman stands over him, a man possessed-

>   BATMAN
>   WHERE ARE THEY?!

He GRABS the Joker, holding him close-

>   THE JOKER
>   Killing is making a choice...

Batman PUNCHES the Joker across the face. HARD.

>   BATMAN
>   *WHERE ARE THEY?!*

The Joker FEEDS off Batman's anger. Loving it.

>   THE JOKER
>   ...you choose one life over the
>   other. Your friend, the district
>   attorney. Or his blushing bride-
>   to-be.

Batman PUNCHES the Joker again. The Joker LAUGHS.

>   THE JOKER (CONT'D)
>   You have *nothing*. Nothing to
>   threaten me with. Nothing to do
>   with all your strength...
>   (spits a tooth)
>   But don't worry, I'm going to tell
>   you where they are. Both of them,
>   and that's the point- you'll have
>   to *choose*.

The Batman stares at the Joker...

>   THE JOKER (CONT'D)
>   *He's* at 250 52nd Boulevard. And
>   *she's* on avenue X at Cicero.

Batman DROPS him.

INT. OBSERVATION ROOM, MCU, GOTHAM CENTRAL -- NIGHT

Batman RACES past Gordon.

                    GORDON
          Which one are you-

                    BATMAN
          Dent knew the risks.

Gordon looks back- the Joker is bloody, but grinning.

EXT. MCU, GOTHAM CENTRAL -- NIGHT

Several cops see Batman climb onto the bat-pod and TEAR
off.

EXT. STREETS, GOTHAM -- NIGHT

Batman SWERVES into oncoming traffic, CHAOS in his wake.

EXT. GOTHAM CENTRAL -- NIGHT

Gordon and his men SCRAMBLE into their cars...

INT. BASEMENT APARTMENT -- NIGHT

Black.

                    RACHEL (O.S.)
          Can anyone hear me?

Harvey Dent opens his eyes. He's bound to a chair in a
dingy, unfurnished basement apartment.

                    DENT
          Rachel? Rachel is that you?

                    RACHEL (O.S.)
               (sobbing)
          Harvey. You're OK. I thought...

Her voice is coming from a speakerphone on the floor.

                    DENT
          It's OK, Rachel. Everything's
          going to be just fine.

He looks around. Behind him, metal BARRELS, hooked up to a
car battery, with a TIMER counting down: five minutes.

INT. INTERROGATION ROOM, MCU, GOTHAM CENTRAL -- NIGHT

The Joker sits, smiling, content. Stephens guards the
door.

> THE JOKER
> I want my phone call.

> STEPHENS
> That's nice.

> THE JOKER
> How many of your friends have I
> killed?

> STEPHENS
> I'm a twenty year man. I can tell
> the difference between punks who
> need a little lesson in manners,
> and the freaks like you who would
> just enjoy it.
> (quiet)
> And you killed six of my friends.

INT. HOLDING AREA, MCU, GOTHAM CENTRAL -- NIGHT

The Fat Thug shuffles to the bars, where a COP stands
guard.

> FAT THUG
> (agony)
> Please. My insides hurt.

> COP
> Step away from the bars.

> FAT THUG
> The boss said he would make the
> voices go away. He said he would
> go inside and replace them with
> bright lights. Like Christmas.

> COP
> That's great. Please step-

The Fat Thug COLLAPSES. The Cop grabs his radio.

INT. WAREHOUSE -- NIGHT

Rachel is bound to a chair. Behind her are barrels
identical to the ones behind Dent.

                    DENT (O.S.)
            Can you move your chair?

                    RACHEL
            No. Harvey, we don't have much
            time-

The timer connected to the bomb reads *2.47... 2.46...*

INT. BASEMENT APARTMENT -- NIGHT

Dent DRAGS his chair, inching closer to the barrels.

                    DENT
            Look for something to free
            yourself.

The chair JAMS against a ridge in the floor. Dent STRAINS
to reach the timer. Inches shy.

                    RACHEL (O.S.)
            They said only one of us was going
            to make it. That they'd let our...
                (pause)
            Our friends choose...

Dent strains... THE CHAIR, AND DENT, TOPPLE OVER- KNOCKING
OVER A BARREL.

                    RACHEL (O.S.) (CONT'D)
            Harvey? What's happening?

Dent, one side of his face pressed against the bare floor,
watches the open barrel SPEW DIESEL FUEL around him-

                    DENT
            Nothing. I'm trying to...

Dent contorts his head to keep from swallowing any.

EXT. STREETS, GOTHAM -- NIGHT

The bat-pod SKIDS SIDEWAYS, WHEELS FLIPPING as the gyro
keeps Batman upright on the tumbling bike- it comes to
rest- guns lined up with a fire exit- BLOWS the door off
its hinges- JUMPS off the bike-

EXT. 52ND STREET, GOTHAM -- NIGHT

Gridlock. Gordon SWERVES onto the sidewalk. People
SCATTER.

INT. INTERROGATION ROOM, MCU, GOTHAM CENTRAL -- NIGHT

The Joker sits like a kid kept after class. He smiles.

                    THE JOKER
          You know why I use a knife,
          Detective? Guns are too quick.
          You don't get to savor all the
          little emotions. See, in their
          last moments, people show you who
          they really are...

Stephens tries hard to ignore him. It isn't working.

                    THE JOKER (CONT'D)
          So, in a way, I knew your friends
          better than you ever did.
               (smiles)
          Would you like to know which of
          them were really cowards?

                    STEPHENS
               (rolls up sleeves)
          I know you're going to enjoy this.
          But I'm going to enjoy it more.

Stephens PUNCHES the Joker in the gut.

INT. BASEMENT APARTMENT -- NIGHT

Dent is half submerged in diesel fuel.

                    RACHEL
          Harvey, in case... I want you to
          know something...

Dent CHOKES, his emotions overwhelming him.

                    DENT
          Don't think like that, Rachel.
          They're coming for you.

                    RACHEL
          I know, but I don't want them to...

INT. WAREHOUSE -- NIGHT

Rachel looks at the timer. Ten seconds left.

>
>   RACHEL
>   I don't want to live without you.
>   Because I do have an answer, and my
>   answer is *yes*...

INT. HOLDING AREA, MCU, GOTHAM CENTRAL -- NIGHT

A MEDIC CUTS away the Fat Thug's shirt- his belly has large
INCISION, which has been closed with crude looking
STITCHES-

>   MEDIC
>   He's got some kind of...
>   contusion...

A RECTANGULAR SHAPE is visible under the skin above his
navel.

INT. DETECTIVE'S ROOM, MCU, GOTHAM CENTRAL -- NIGHT

Stephens shuffles out into the room, a piece of BROKEN
GLASS held to his THROAT by the Joker. Cops draw their
weapons.

>   STEPHENS
>   This is my own damn fault. Just
>   shoot him.

>   DETECTIVE MURPHY
>   What do you want?

>   THE JOKER
>   I want my phone call.

The Detectives look at each other. One of them pulls out
his cell phone. TOSSES it to the Joker, who begins to
dial.

INT. HOLDING AREA, MCU, GOTHAM CENTRAL -- NIGHT

The Medic gingerly PRESSES the rectangle. It illuminates,
a soft blue light visible through the skin.

>   COP
>   Is that a... *phone*?

INT. DETECTIVE'S ROOM, MCU, GOTHAM CENTRAL -- NIGHT

The Joker presses SEND. At the end of the room, the door to the holding area EXPLODES-

INT. HALLWAY, TENEMENT -- NIGHT

Batman SPRINTS down the hall- stops at a door- KICKS it-

EXT. 52ND STREET, GOTHAM -- NIGHT

Cars PULL UP- Gordon gets out, carrying a fire ax-

INT. HALLWAY, TENEMENT -- NIGHT

Batman KICKS- the door gives- Batman SMASHES it open-

INT. BASEMENT APARTMENT -- NIGHT

...Batman BURSTS through the door- Dent looks up in horror-

> DENT
> NO! *Not me*... Why did you come for *me*?!

Batman STARES at Dent. The Joker lied. The counter hits 5 seconds. Batman DRAGS Dent out- Dent FIGHTS to stay-

> DENT (CONT'D)
> RACHEL!

> RACHEL (O.S.)
> *Harvey? Harvey, it's okay...*

> DENT
> RACHEL!!!

EXT. 52ND STREET, GOTHAM -- NIGHT

Gordon, axe in hand, RUNS towards the entrance-

INT. WAREHOUSE -- NIGHT

Rachel can hear Dent. The counter runs out.

> RACHEL
> (calm)
> Somewhere-

AN EXPLOSION. ALL-CONSUMING.

EXT. 52ND STREET, GOTHAM -- NIGHT

The BLAST HURLS Gordon backward onto the hood of his car-
THE ENTIRE WAREHOUSE IS AN ENORMOUS EXPLOSION-

INT. BASEMENT APARTMENT -- NIGHT

Batman wraps his cape around Dent and hurls them both
through the door. Dent is SCREAMING-

EXT. 52ND STREET, GOTHAM -- NIGHT

Gordon picks himself up. The warehouse is an inferno. He
heads for it anyway. Five of his men have to RESTRAIN HIM.

EXT. ALLEYWAY, GOTHAM -- NIGHT

A SECOND EXPLOSION- Batman COVERS Dent as the FIREBALL HITS
them- IGNITING the diesel soaking Dent's left side- he
starts BURNING. And stops screaming. Batman ROLLS Dent on
the wet pavement... Dent SIZZLES. Silent.

INT. SPECIAL HOLDING AREA, MCU, GOTHAM CENTRAL -- NIGHT

The Joker walks to the bars of another cell. Grins.

                    THE JOKER
              Hello there.

In his cell. Terrified. Lau.

EXT. AMBULANCE -- CONTINUOUS

Dent is wheeled into an ambulance, bandages held to his
face. His one visible eye STARES BLANKLY, oblivious to the
panic-

EXT. 52ND STREET -- CONTINUOUS

Gordon watches the fire. DEBRIS blows across the asphalt.
Gordon picks up two pieces: SINGED JOKER CARDS. In place
of the Joker's face is a PHOTO OF LAU. A POLICE SERGEANT
approaches.

                    SERGEANT
              Dent's alive, Jim. Just. But back
              at M.C.U.... the Joker's gone...
                    GORDON
              With Lau?

>   (the Cop nods)
>   The Joker *planned* to be caught.   He
>   wanted me to lock him up in M.C.U..

EXT. STREET, DOWNTOWN GOTHAM -- DAWN

A squad car BLAZES down the street. The Joker sticks his
head out the window like a dog, feeling the wind...

INT. KITCHEN, WAYNE PENTHOUSE -- DAWN

Alfred sits at a table reading the letter from Rachel.

>   RACHEL (V.O.)
>   *Dear Bruce, I need to explain...*

EXT. 52ND STREET -- DAWN

Water. Smoldering blackness. The FIRE CREWS extinguish
the last flames of the devastated building. A FIREMAN
nudges his COLLEAGUE, pointing out something in the
devastation...

>   *RACHEL*
>   *...I need to be honest and clear.*
>   *I'm going to marry Harvey Dent...*

INT. INTENSIVE CARE UNIT -- DAWN

Glimpses of Dent's damaged face as SURGEONS surround him.

>   *RACHEL (V.O.)*
>   *I love him, I want to spend the*
>   *rest of my life with him...*

EXT. 52ND STREET -- DAWN

The Firemen watch a statue-like figure amidst the charred
ruins. The Batman.

>   *RACHEL (V.O.)*
>   *When I told you that if Gotham no*
>   *longer needed Batman we could be*
>   *together, I meant it...*

INT. MCU, GOTHAM CENTRAL -- DAY

Gordon surveys the wreckage of MCU. The bodies.

>   *RACHEL (V.O.)*

                    But I'm not sure the day will
                    come...

EXT. 52ND STREET -- DAWN

Batman bends to the ground on one knee, his black glove
spread against the smoldering debris.

                         RACHEL (V.O.)
                    ...when you no longer need Batman.
                    I hope it does, and if it does I
                    will be there...

He spots something. DENT'S TWO-HEADED COIN. Blackened,
SCARRED. Batman turns it over. The other side is
PRISTINE.

INT. KITCHEN, WAYNE PENTHOUSE -- DAWN

Alfred reads.

                         RACHEL (V.O.)
                    ...but as your friend. I'm sorry
                    to let you down...

INT. HOSPITAL ROOM -- DAWN

Dent, heavily bandaged, hooked up to various machines.
Batman stands at the foot of his bed. Watching.

                         RACHEL
                    If you lose your faith in me,
                    please keep your faith in people...

                         BATMAN
                    I'm sorry, Harvey.

Batman puts DENT'S DAMAGED COIN on the bedside table.

INT. KITCHEN, WAYNE PENTHOUSE -- CONTINUOUS

                         RACHEL (V.O.)
                    Love, now and always, Rachel.

Alfred finishes the letter. Tears in his eyes, he folds it
back into its envelope. Places it on the breakfast tray.

INT. WAYNE PENTHOUSE -- DAWN

Alfred moves through the silent space, stepping past the cowl and gauntlets lying on the cold marble. He approaches Wayne, half-undressed, slumped in a chair watching Gotham.

                    ALFRED
          I prepared a little breakfast.

Nothing. Alfred sets down the tray. The envelope is propped against the silver teapot.

                    ALFRED (CONT'D)
          Very well.

                    WAYNE
          Alfred?

                    ALFRED
          Yes, Master Wayne?

Wayne turns, a desperate look in his eye.

                    WAYNE
          Did I bring this on us? On her? I
          thought I would inspire good, not
          madness-

                    ALFRED
          You *have* inspired good. But you
          spat in the face of Gotham's
          criminals- didn't you think there
          might be casualties? Things were
          always going to have to get worse
          before they got better.

                    WAYNE
          But *Rachel*, Alfred...

                    ALFRED
          Rachel believed in what you stood
          for. What *we* stand for.

Wayne looks up at Alfred. Alfred picks up the cowl.

                    ALFRED (CONT'D)
          Gotham needs you.

                    WAYNE
          Gotham needs its hero. And I let
          the Joker blow him half to hell-

                         ALFRED
              Which is why for now, they'll have
              to make do with *you*.

Alfred hands him the cowl. Wayne looks at him.

                         WAYNE
              She was going to wait for me. Dent
              doesn't know. He can *never* know...

Alfred glances at the envelope. Takes it off the tray.

                         WAYNE (CONT'D)
              What's that?

                         ALFRED
              It can wait.

Alfred puts the envelope in his pocket.

                         WAYNE
              That bandit, in the forest in
              Burma... Did you catch him?
                   (Alfred nods)
              How?

                         ALFRED
                   (uneasy)
              We burned the forest down.

EXT. DOWNTOWN GOTHAM -- DAY

A national guard helicopter ROARS over Gotham General.

INT. HOSPITAL ROOM -- DAY

Dent. Bandaged. Sedated. Coming up for air. Sees
something on the table: his coin. He fumbles for it,
marvelling at its shiny face. Remembering.

INSERT CUT: RACHEL CATCHES THE COIN.

Dent turns the coin over. The other side is devastated.
He STARES at the scarred face. Starts ripping his
bandages.

INT. WAYNE PENTHOUSE -- DAY

Alfred comes up to Wayne. Points him to the TV.

                    ALFRED
          You need to see this.

On screen: *Engel, in his studio, addresses the camera.*

                    ENGEL
          ...he's a credible source- an A and
          M lawyer for a prestigious
          consultancy. He says he's waited
          as long as he can for the Batman to
          do the right thing...

The shot cuts to REESE, nodding.

                    ENGEL (CONT'D)
          Now he's taking matters into his
          own hands. We'll be live at five
          with the true identity of the
          Batman, stay with us...

INT. HOSPITAL ROOM -- CONTINUOUS

Gordon ENTERS. Dent STARES to one side. He looks normal.

                    GORDON
          I'm sorry about Rachel.
              (nothing)
          The Doctor says you're in agonizing
          pain but you won't accept
          medication. That you're refusing
          skin grafts-

                    DENT
          Remember the name you all had for
          me when I was at Internal Affairs?
          What was it, Gordon?

                    GORDON
          Harvey, I can't-

                    DENT
          SAY IT!

Dent's anger makes Gordon flinch. He looks away. Ashamed.

                    GORDON
              (small)
          Two-face. Harvey two-face.

Dent turns to face Gordon- the left side of Dent's face is
DESTROYED- skin blackened and shriveled. Molars visible.
The eye a ball and socket. Dent manages a small smile with
the good side of his face.

                    DENT
          Why should I hide who I am?

                    GORDON
          I... I know you tried to warn me.
          I'm sorry. Wuertz picked you up-
          was he working for them?
               (nothing)
          Do you know who picked up Rachel?
               (nothing)
          Harvey, I need to know which of my
          men I can trust.

Dent looks at Gordon. Cold.

                    DENT
          Why would you listen to me *now*?

                    GORDON
          I'm sorry, Harvey.

                    DENT
          No. No you're not. Not yet.

Gordon takes a last look at Dent. Then leaves.

INT. CORRIDOR, HOSPITAL -- CONTINUOUS

Gordon steps out. Someone is there. Maroni. On crutches.
Gordon stares at him. Cold. Maroni shifts, awkward.

                    MARONI
          This craziness. This is too much.

                    GORDON
          You should have thought of that
          before you let the clown out of the
          box.

                    MARONI
          You want him, I can tell you where
          he'll be this afternoon.

EXT. ABANDONED DOCKS -- DAY

The Chechen gets out of his SUV. Looks at a RUSTED HULK.
The Chechen, bodyguards, and dogs, head up the gangplank.

INT. RUSTED HULK -- CONTINUOUS

They pass into a huge hold. In the middle: A BILLION
DOLLARS. The pile is thirty feet high. Standing on top-
the Joker. At his feet, bound, is Lau. The Chechen
laughs.

> CHECHEN
> Like I say- not so crazy as you
> look.

The Joker jumps from the top, slides down the pile.

> THE JOKER
> I told you- I'm a man of my word.
> (looks around)
> Where's the Italian?

The Chechen shrugs. Pulls out a cigar. Lights it.

> CHECHEN
> More for us. What you do with all
> your money, Mr.Joker?

The Joker GRABS a can of GASOLINE from his thug.

> THE JOKER
> I'm a man of simple tastes. I like
> gunpowder. Dynamite...

He is SPLASHING gasoline onto the money.

> THE JOKER (CONT'D)
> ...*gasoline*...

The Chechen, FURIOUS, steps forwards. The Joker turns.
JABS his gun in the Chechen's face. The Chechen's
bodyguards REACT. The Joker's men DRAW on them.

> THE JOKER (CONT'D)
> And you know what they have in
> common? They're *cheap.*

> CHECHEN
> You said you were a man of your
> word.

The Joker PLUCKS the cigar from the Chechen's lips.

                    THE JOKER
          I am.

The Joker tosses the cigar at the pile.

                    THE JOKER (CONT'D)
          I'm only burning *my* half.

The Chechen watches the money catch fire.

                    THE JOKER (CONT'D)
          All you care about is money. This
          city deserves a better class of
          criminal, and I'm going to give it
          to them. This is my town now.
          Tell your men they work for me.

The Joker crouches down to the Chechen's dogs. They GROWL.

                    CHECHEN
          They won't work for a freak.

The Joker takes out a knife. Tosses it to his man.

                    THE JOKER
          Cut him up and offer him to his
          little Princes. Let's show him
          just how loyal a hungry dog is.

The Joker's men GRAB the Chechen.

                    THE JOKER (CONT'D)
          It's not about money. It's about
          sending a message...

The Joker watches the towering FLAMES. Lau screams.

                    THE JOKER (CONT'D)
          Everything. Burns.

The Joker pulls out a phone...

INT. TELEVISION STUDIO -- DAY

Reese has a confident air. Engel is taking calls.

                    CALLER 1 (O.S.)

I wanna how much they're gonna pay
you to say who Batman really is.

                    REESE
That's simply not why I'm doing
this.

                    ENGEL
Caller, you're on the air.

                    CALLER 2 (O.S.)
Harvey dent didn't want us to give
in to this maniac- you think you
know better than him?

                    ENGEL
Guy's got a point- Dent didn't want
Batman to give himself up, is this
the right thing to do?

                    REESE
If we could talk to Dent now he
might feel differently-

                    ENGEL
And we wish him a speedy recovery.
God knows we need him, now. Let's
take another call-

                    OLD LADY (O.S.)
Mr.Reese, what's more valuable: one
life, or a hundred?

                    REESE
I guess it would depend on the
life.

                    OLD LADY (O.S.)
OK. Let's say it's your life. Is
it worth more than the lives of
several hundred others?

                    REESE
Of course not.

                    OLD LADY (O.S.)
I'm glad you feel that way.
Because I've put a bomb in one of
the city's hospitals. It's going

off in sixty minutes unless someone
kills you.

                    ENGEL
Who is this?

                    OLD LADY (O.S.)
Just a concerned citizen-
        (drops pitch to the
         JOKER'S VOICE)
-and regular guy...

INT. MAJOR CRIMES UNIT, GOTHAM CENTRAL -- CONTINUOUS

Gordon and his men are gearing up to take down the Joker.
A Detective turns up the TV in the bullpen-

                    THE JOKER (O.S.)
I had a vision. Of a world without
Batman. The mob ground out a
little profit and the police tried
to shut them down, one block at a
time... and it was so... boring.
I've had a change of heart. I
don't want Mr.Reese spoiling
everything, but why should I have
all the fun? Let's give someone
else a chance...

Reese looks around, twitching. Sweating.

                    THE JOKER (O.S.) (CONT'D)
If Coleman Reese isn't dead in
sixty minutes, then I blow up a
hospital. Of course, you could
always kill yourself, Mr.Reese.
But that would be the noble thing
to do. And you're a lawyer.

The line rings off. Engel is speechless.

Gordon turns to the uniform COPS.

                    GORDON
Call in every officer- tell them to
head to their nearest hospital and
start evac and search. Call the
transit authority, school board,
prisons- get every available bus

down to a hospital- the priority is
Gotham General- wheel everybody out
of that place right now- my hunch
is that's where the bomb is.

                    DETECTIVE MURPHY
          Why?

                    GORDON
          That's where Harvey Dent is.

The Uniforms SPRINT off. Gordon turns to his Detectives.

                    UNIFORMED COP
          Where are we going, sir?

On screen: Reese is a deer in the headlights.

                    GORDON
          To get Reese.

INT. WAYNE PENTHOUSE -- DAY

Wayne and Alfred move to the elevator.

                    WAYNE
          I need you plugged in, checking
          Gordon's men and their families.

                    ALFRED
          Looking for?

                    WAYNE
          Hospital admissions.

                    ALFRED
          Will you be taking the batpod, sir?

                    WAYNE
          In the middle of the day? Not very
          subtle, Alfred.

                    ALFRED
          The Lamborghini then.
             (watches Wayne go)
          Much more subtle.

EXT. GOTHAM STREETS -- DAY

Wayne's Lamborghini TEARS through downtown.

INT. HOSPITAL -- CONTINUOUS

CHAOS. PATIENTS and STAFF running around. COPS and
TRAFFIC WARDENS try to manage the evacuation. The COPS
stationed outside Dent's room, look around, unsure-

                    NURSE
          Sir, are you going to help?!

Two Cops move to help wheel gurneys around the corner.

OMITTED

INT. LOBBY, TELEVISION STUDIO -- DAY

Gordon and his men escort Reese out of the elevator- Engel
follows with a camera crew. As they approach the glass
doors Gordon looks out at an angry crowd.

                    ENGEL
          Commissioner?! You really think
          someone would try to-

Gordon SPOTS an OLD MAN raising a PISTOL- Gordon THROWS
Reese to the ground as SHOTS SHATTER the laminated glass of
the lobby. The Crowd SURGES in all directions-

                    GORDON
          Get the cars around back!

Gordon hauls Reese to the stairwell.

INT. LAMBORGHINI -- CONTINUOUS

Wayne SLOWS past the chaos outside the television station.

                    WAYNE
          I saw O'Brien and Richards...

INT. BAT-BUNKER -- CONTINUOUS

Alfred types at the computer station.

                    ALFRED (O.S.)
          Nothing on them. No immediate
          family members admitted to a Gotham
          hospital.

INT. STAIRWELL, TELEVISION STUDIO -- CONTINUOUS

Gordon pulls the shaken Reese down the stairs...

                    REESE
               (shaken)
          They're trying to kill me.

...and into a police VAN...

INT. POLICE VAN -- CONTINUOUS

Gordon throws Reese in the back.   Smiles.

                    GORDON
          Well, maybe Batman will save you.

The van PEELS out.   Heads onto the streets.

EXT. HOSPITAL -- CONTINUOUS

Cops load patients onto BUSES.   A TV van pulls up, Engel
and his Cameraman jump out.   One of Dent's guards, POLK,
looks into a SCHOOL BUS.   Turns to the Cop loading it.

                    POLK
          Okay, don't put anyone else on.
               (gets on radio)
          Davis, I got space, bring him out.
               (no answer)
          Davis?

Polk heads back towards the hospital, against the flow.

INT. LAMBORGHINI -- CONTINUOUS

Wayne trails the police van from a distance.

                    WAYNE
          I saw Burns and Zachary... and a
          patrolman I don't know.

                    ALFRED (O.S.)
          Burns is clean... Zachary...

                    WAYNE
          There's at least one I don't know-
          send the information to Gordon-

INT. POLICE VAN -- CONTINUOUS

Gordon's phone BEEPS. He looks at a text: *WATCH OUT. COPS WITH RELATIVES IN GOTHAM HOSPITALS- BURKE, RAMIREZ, TILL...*

INT. DENT'S HOSPITAL ROOM -- CONTINUOUS

Polk enters the room. No Davis. Just a REDHEADED NURSE, back towards him, reading Dent's chart.

                  POLK
      Ma'am, we're going to have to move
      him, now.
           (nothing)
      Ma'am?

The Redhead TURNS- it is the Joker, silenced pistol in hand. He FIRES.

EXT. GOTHAM STREETS -- CONTINUOUS

The Lamborghini zips around a car to get closer to the van.

INT. POLICE VAN -- CONTINUOUS

Gordon is reading his phone: *ERIKSON, BERG.* Gordon looks up sharply. Considers the uniformed cop nervously fingering his shotgun.

                GORDON
      Berg, isn't it?

The young cop, BERG, looks up. Sweating.

                BERG
      Commissioner?

                GORDON
      You okay, son?

Berg nods. Looks at his watch.

INT. HOSPITAL ROOM -- DAY

The Joker draws closer to Dent's bed. Dent STRAINS at the leather cuffs binding him to the bed.

              THE JOKER
      I don't want there to be any hard
      feelings between us, Harvey.

The Joker loosens Dent's restraints.

                    THE JOKER (CONT'D)
          When you and Rachel were being
          abducted I was sitting in Gordon's
          cage. I didn't rig those charges-

                    DENT
          Your men. Your plan.

                    THE JOKER
          Do I really look like a guy with a
          plan, Harvey? I don't have a
          plan...

                    THE JOKER (CONT'D)
          The mob has plans, the cops have
          plans. You know what I am, Harvey?

Dent's hand is TREMBLING.

                    THE JOKER (CONT'D)
          I'm a dog chasing cars... I
          wouldn't know what to do with one
          if I caught it. I just *do* things.
          I'm just the wrench in the gears.
          I hate plans. Yours, theirs,
          everyone's. Maroni has plans.
          Gordon has plans. Schemers trying
          to control their worlds. I'm not a
          schemer, I show the schemers how
          pathetic their attempts to control
          things really are. So when I say
          that you and your girlfriend was
          nothing personal, you know *I'm*
          telling the truth...

Hands him the pistol. Dent holds it to the Joker's head.

EXT. INTERSECTION, GOTHAM STREETS -- CONTINUOUS

Wayne ROARS past a line of traffic to settle in a few cars
back from the police van, sitting at a red light.

INT. LAMBORGHINI -- CONTINUOUS

Wayne studies the intersection- spots a PICKUP jostling for
position on the cross street.

INT. POLICE VAN -- CONTINUOUS

Gordon watches Berg, mentally tracing the trajectory of his shotgun barrel as Berg fiddles with his gun. Gordon starts trying to subtly unholster his own weapon.

> GORDON
> I'm gonna need your weapon, son.

Berg looks at Gordon.

> BERG
> What?

INT. LAMBORGHINI -- CONTINUOUS

Wayne watches the driver of the pickup staring intently at the police van. Lining it up.

INT. POLICE VAN -- CONTINUOUS

Reese looks from Berg to Gordon. Berg looks at Gordon, trembling, the barrel of his gun inching lower in the car.

> BERG
> Why? Because my wife's in hospital?

> GORDON
> Yeah. That would be why.

INT. DENT'S HOSPITAL ROOM -- CONTINUOUS

The Joker leans in, pressing his head to the gun's barrel.

> THE JOKER
> It's the schemers who put you where you are. *You* were a schemer. You had plans. Look where it got you. I just did what I do best- I took your plan, and I turned it on itself. Look what I've done to this city with a few drums of gas and a couple of bullets. Nobody panics when the *expected* people get killed. Nobody panics when things go according to plan, even if the plan is horrifying. If I tell the press that tomorrow a gangbanger will get shot, or a truckload of soldiers will be blown up, nobody panics. Because it's all part of

                    the plan. But when I say that one
                    little old mayor will die,
                    everybody loses their minds!
                    Introduce a little anarchy, you
                    upset the established order and
                    everything becomes chaos. I'm an
                    agent of chaos. And you know the
                    thing about chaos, Harvey?

Dent looks into the Joker's eyes. Finding meaning.

                         THE JOKER (CONT'D)
                    It's *fair.*

Dent looks down at the coin in his hands. Turns it over,
feels it's comforting weight. Shows the Joker the good
side.

                         DENT
                    You live.

He turns the coin over. The flip side is deeply SCARRED.

                         DENT (CONT'D)
                    You die.

The Joker looks at the coin. Looks at Dent, admiringly.

                         THE JOKER
                    Now you're talking.

Dent FLICKS the coin into the air. Catches it. Looks.

EXT. INTERSECTION, GOTHAM STREETS -- CONTINUOUS

The light turns GREEN. The police van pulls into the
intersection- the pickup GUNS IT, RACING AT IT...

INT. LAMBORGHINI -- CONTINUOUS

Wayne FLOORS it, YANKS the wheel to pull up onto the
sidewalk-

INT. POLICE VAN -- CONTINUOUS

Berg licks his lips, nervous.

                         BERG
                    Mr.Reese?

EXT. INTERSECTION, GOTHAM STREETS -- CONTINUOUS

The pickup BARRELS at the van, FULL TILT- at the last
second Wayne's Lamborghini SLIPS alongside the van- the
pickup SMASHES INTO THE LAMBORGHINI-

INT. POLICE VAN -- CONTINUOUS

As the van JOLTS with the impact Gordon LEAPS forward,
PUSHING UP Berg's shotgun barrel, which FIRES into the
roof- Gordon SMASHES Berg on the head with his sidearm.

EXT. INTERSECTION, GOTHAM STREETS -- CONTINUOUS

Gordon's men pull the pickup driver from his cab- Gordon
crouches down to the Lamborghini wreck to help pull Wayne
from the car. Gordon recognizes him as he pulls him free.

                    GORDON
          You okay, Mr.Wayne?

Wayne looks at him, woozy. Sits on the curb.

                    WAYNE
          Call me Bruce. I think so.

                    GORDON
          That was a brave thing, you did.

                    WAYNE
          Trying to catch the light?

                    GORDON
          You weren't protecting the van?

Wayne turns- sees the police van as if for the first time.
Reese steps down, dazed.

                    WAYNE
          Why? Who's in it?

Reese locks eyes with Wayne. Nods. Gordon sizes up Bruce
Wayne and his crushed sports car.

                    GORDON
          You don't watch a whole lot of
          news, do you, Mr.Wayne?

                    WAYNE
               (shrugs)

It can get a little intense. Think
I should go to hospital?

              GORDON
Not today, I wouldn't.

INT. CORRIDOR, HOSPITAL -- CONTINUOUS

The Joker walks calmly through the mostly deserted
building. As he walks he pulls a DETONATOR from his
pocket. Strolling along he PUSHES THE BUTTON... STAGGERED
EXPLOSIONS BURST INTO THE CORRIDOR BEHIND HIM LIKE
DEMOLITION BLASTS... the Joker just walks out the door...

EXT. HOSPITAL -- CONTINUOUS

The Joker STROLLS down the steps- WINDOWS BLOW OUT IN
SERIES- People DIVE for cover- Engel PILES into a school
bus-

The Joker walks across the parking lot- THE BUILDING
COLLAPSING BEHIND HIM...

EXT. INTERSECTION, GOTHAM STREETS -- CONTINUOUS

Gordon hears the EXPLOSION.

              GORDON
Gotham general...
    (grabs his phone)
Did you get Dent out?

             COP (O.S.)
I think so-

EXT. HOSPITAL -- CONTINUOUS

The Cop cowers as DEBRIS and SMOKE BLAST across the street-

INT. SCHOOL BUS -- CONTINUOUS

The Joker gets onto the bus. Nods at his man at the wheel.

EXT. HOSPITAL -- CONTINUOUS

All eyes are on the collapsed building. One school bus
pulls out from the line of other buses. Heads down the
street.

INT. BAR, GOTHAM HEIGHTS -- DAY

An empty neighborhood dive, the local DRUNK passed out at
the bar, BARTENDER, watching BREAKING NEWS on the TV.

                    BARTENDER
          Sweet Jesus. D'you see this, Mike?
          They blew up a hospital...

Detective Wuertz, at a booth looks up at the TV, bored.

                    BARTENDER (CONT'D)
          Shouldn't you be out there, you
          know, doing something?

                    WUERTZ
          It's my day off.

The Bartender shuts the register.

                    BARTENDER
          I gotta take a leak, keep an eye on
          things, will ya?

The Bartender steps out. The back door OPENS again.

                    WUERTZ
          What? You need me to shake it for-

He TRAILS off as someone sticks a gun in his face: Harvey
Dent. Standing in shadow. He sits.

                    DENT
          Hello.

                    WUERTZ
          Dent, I thought you was... dead...

Dent leans into the light. The left side of his face is
HIDEOUSLY BURNED, cheek gone, blackened teeth and gums.

                    DENT
          Half.

Dent picks up Wuertz's drink. Takes a SIP. Wuertz watches
the bare muscles RETRACT as Dent SWALLOWS.

                    DENT (CONT'D)
          Who picked up Rachel, Wuertz?

                    WUERTZ
          It must've been Maroni's men-

Dent SLAMS the glass back on the table- Wuertz FLINCHES.

                    DENT
          You, of all people, are gonna
          protect the other traitor in
          Gordon's unit?

                    WUERTZ
          I don't know- he'd never tell *me*.

                    WUERTZ
              (stares at Dent)
          I swear to God, I didn't know what
          they were gonna do to you-

                    DENT
          Funny, I don't know what's going to
          happen to you, either.

Dent pulls his coin from his pocket. FLIPS it. Wuertz
watches it SPIN. It lands on the table. Scarred side up.
The drunk at the bar STIRS at the GUNSHOT.

EXT. GOTHAM GENERAL -- DAY

Gordon, manic, surveys the scene with a Cop-

                    GORDON
          You must know how many were inside-
          you've got patient lists, roll
          calls-

                    COP
          Sir! Sir. Take a look at what
          we're dealing with. Cops, National
          Guard-
              (gestures at buses)
          We're showing 50 missing- but that
          building was clear. These buses
          are heading off to other hospitals-
          my guess is we missed one.

                    GORDON
          Yeah? What's your *guess* about
          where Harvey Dent is?

The cop says nothing.

                    GORDON (CONT'D)
          Keep looking. Keep it to yourself.

INT. FOX'S OFFICE WAYNE INDUSTRIES -- DAY

Fox is watching the news. His intercom buzzes.

                    VOICE (O.S.)
          Mr.Fox? Security is showing a
          break-in at the R and D department.

INT. CORRIDOR OUTSIDE RESEARCH AND DEVELOPMENT -- DAY

Fox watches two security men force the door. He enters
alone.

INT. LAB, RESEARCH AND DEVELOPMENT -- DAY

Fox enters the dimly-lit room. At one end is an
extraordinary array of thousands of tiny monitors. Fox
approaches, fascinated, as they quietly display
architectural patterns individually and in concert. The
images become a MAP.

                    BATMAN (O.S.)
          Beautiful. Isn't it?

Fox nods, staring at the monitors as Batman approaches.

                    FOX
          Beautiful. Unethical. *Dangerous.*
          You've turned every phone in the
          city into a microphone...

Lucius presses a key. The BABBLE of a MILLION
CONVERSATIONS at once fills the room. Every cell phone in
the city.

                    BATMAN
          And high frequency
          generator/receiver.

                    FOX
          Like the phone I gave you in Hong
          Kong. You took my sonar concept
          and applied it to everybody's phone
          in the City. With half the city
          feeding you sonar you can image all
          of Gotham.
               (turns to Batman)
          This is *wrong.*

                    BATMAN

                    I've got to find this man, Lucius.

                              FOX
                    But at what cost?

                              BATMAN
                    The database is null-key encrypted.
                    It can only be accessed by one
                    person.

                              FOX
                    No one should have that kind of
                    power.

                              WAYNE
                    That's why I gave it to you. Only
                    you can use it.

Lucius looks at Batman. Hard.

                              FOX
                    Spying on thirty million people
                    wasn't in my job description.

Batman points to a TV screen. Fox turns. ON SCREEN: *the
Joker shakes his head above a graphic "LATEST THREAT"*...

                              THE JOKER
                    What does it take to make you
                    people want to join in..?

EXT. SITUATION TENT AT GOTHAM GENERAL -- CONTINUOUS

Gordon watches a screen. Grave.

                              THE JOKER
                    You failed to kill the lawyer...
                    I've got to get you off the bench
                    and into the game. So, here it
                    is...

INT. BAR, DOWNTOWN -- CONTINUOUS

The bar, packed with business people watches the TV.
SILENT.

                              THE JOKER
                    Come nightfall, this city is mine,
                    and anyone left here plays by my

>   *rules. If you don't want to be in*
>   *the game, get out now.*

Bar patrons start moving... *The Joker reaches for the camera-*

>   THE JOKER (CONT'D)
>   *But the bridge-and-tunnel crowd are*
>   *in for a surprise.*

CUT TO STATIC. The bar patrons look around, confused.

INT. LAB, RESEARCH AND DEVELOPMENT -- CONTINUOUS

Fox turns from the TV to look at Batman.

>   BATMAN
>   Trust me.

Fox stares at Batman.

>   BATMAN (CONT'D)
>   This is the audio sample.

He plugs a USB dongle into the console. A sample of the Joker's voice from the call-in news program plays.

>   BATMAN (CONT'D)
>   If he talks within range of any
>   phone in the city, you'll be able
>   to triangulate his position.

Lucius toggles a menu. The city is an open book- People working, eating, sleeping. Lucius shakes his head.

>   BATMAN (CONT'D)
>   When you've finished, type your
>   name to switch it off.

>   FOX
>   I'll help you this one time...

Lucius sits at the console. Batman moves off-

>   FOX (CONT'D)
>   But consider this my resignation.

Batman turns. Fox looks at him, serious.

>   FOX (CONT'D)

As long as this machine is at Wayne
Industries, I won't be.

EXT. VARIOUS LOCATIONS -- DUSK

Gothamites POUR out of the city, on foot and by car... the
BRIDGES and TUNNELS are deserted, but for BOMB SQUAD search
teams.

INT. CITY HALL -- CONTINUOUS

Gordon briefs the Mayor.

> GORDON
> My officers are going over every
> inch of the tunnels and bridges,
> but with the Joker's threat they're
> not and option.

> MAYOR
> Land routes East?

> GORDON
> Backed up for hours. Which leaves
> the ferries with thirty thousand
> waiting to board. Plus,
> corrections are at capacity, so I
> want to use a ferry to take some
> prisoners off the island.

> MAYOR
> The men you and Dent put away?
> Those aren't people I'm worried
> about.

> GORDON
> You should be- they're the people
> you least want to be stuck with in
> an emergency. Whatever the Joker's
> planning, it's a good bet that
> Harvey's prisoners might be
> involved. I want 'em out of here.

EXT. FERRY TERMINAL -- DUSK

At the ferry terminal, National Guardsman watch over the
THIRTY THOUSAND jostling, scared people waiting to board
the two MASSIVE FERRIES to Seven Sisters. Grumbles turn to

YELLS as 800 PRISONERS are loaded onto a ferry by shotgun-toting CORRECTIONS OFFICERS.

                    CIVILIAN
       That ain't right! We should be on
       that boat.

                 NATIONAL GUARDSMAN
       You want to ride across with them,
       be my guest.

EXT. BROWNSTONE -- DUSK

Maroni climbs into the back of a limo.

INT. LIMO -- DUSK

Maroni settles back into his seat. The car pulls away.

                    MARONI
       Don't stop for lights, cops,
       nothing.

                  DENT (O.S.)
       Going to join your wife?

Maroni STARTS. Someone is in here with him. Harvey Dent-Two Face- leans forward, clutching a pistol.

                 DENT (CONT'D)
       You love her?

                    MARONI
       Yes.

                    DENT
       Can you imagine what it would be
       like to listen to her die?

                    MARONI
       Take it up with the Joker. He
       killed your woman. Made you...
       like this...

                    DENT
       The Joker's just a mad dog. I want
       whoever let him off the *leash*.

Maroni looks at Dent. Worried.

                         DENT (CONT'D)
          I took care of Wuertz, but who was
          your other man inside Gordon's
          unit? Who picked up Rachel? It
          must've been someone she trusted.

                         MARONI
          If I tell you, will you let me go?

                         DENT
          It can't hurt your chances.

                         MARONI
          It was Ramirez.

Pulls out his coin. Dent cocks the pistol...

                         MARONI (CONT'D)
          But you said-

                         DENT
          I said it couldn't hurt your
          chances.

Dent FLIPS it. Looks: good side. He shrugs.

                         DENT (CONT'D)
          Lucky guy.

Maroni looks confused. Dent FLIPS the coin again. Looks
down at the coin. Shakes his head.

                         DENT (CONT'D)
          But *he's* not.

                         MARONI
          Who?

Dent smiles. PUTS HIS SEAT BELT ON.

                         DENT
          Your driver.

Dent presses the barrel of the revolver behind the shadow
of the driver. Maroni LUNGES, SCREAMING. Dent FIRES.

EXT. BRIDGE -- DUSK

The Limo SWERVES off of the bridge, SOARS out over the
canal, and PANCAKES into the RETAINING WALL.

EXT. FERRY TERMINAL -- DUSK

CIVILIANS CRAM their way onto one ferry. Finally, the
COMMANDER of the National Guard unit SIGNALS to his men to
STOP BOARDING and CAST OFF.

The two FERRIES set off across the river, heading for the
lights of the distant shore of the mainland.

INT. BRIDGE, PRISONER FERRY -- NIGHT

The FIRST MATE looks out the window, at the second ferry.
It is DEAD in the WATER. He turns to the PILOT [PRISON
FERRY].

                    FIRST MATE
          They've lost their engines.

                    PILOT [PRISON FERRY]
          Get on the radio and tell 'em we'll
          come back for them once we dump
          these scumbags-

Suddenly, the control panel FLICKERS and DIES.

                    PILOT [PRISON FERRY] (CONT'D)
          Get down to the engine room.

INT. PASSENGER LOUNGE, PRISONER FERRY -- NIGHT

The First Mate skirts around the PRISONERS and CORRECTIONS
OFFICERS...

INT. ACCESS CORRIDOR, PRISONER FERRY -- NIGHT

The First Mate opens the door to the engine room. STOPS.

HUNDREDS OF BARRELS OF DIESEL FUEL. And a small, wrapped
PRESENT, topped with a BOW.

INT. BRIDGE, PRISONER FERRY -- NIGHT

The Pilot [Prison Ferry] is holding the small present. His
radio CRACKLES.

                    PILOT [PASSENGER FERRY] (O.S.)
          Same thing over here- enough diesel
          to blow us sky high. And a
          present.

EXT. ELEVATED ROADWAY, DOWTOWN GOTHAM -- CONTINUOUS

Batman sits on the bat-pod, cape blowing. Listening.

>   BATMAN
>   Fox? There's something going on on
>   the ferries...

INT. PASSENGER LOUNGE, COMMUTER FERRY -- NIGHT

As cold scared Families watch, the NATIONAL GUARD COMMANDER
UNWRAPS that ferry's present. Inside, he finds a crude
REMOTE DETONATOR.

>   NATIONAL GUARD COMMANDER
>   Why would they give us the
>   detonator to our own bomb?

Up in the wiring at the ceiling, a CELL PHONE taped in to
the P.A. rings and answers.

>   *THE JOKER* (O.S.)
>   *Tonight, you're all going to be*
>   *part of a social experiment.*

ON BOTH FERRIES: CIVILIANS, PRISONERS, CREW, AND NATIONAL
GUARDSMEN ALL LISTEN AS THE JOKER'S VOICE RINGS OUT.

INT. LAB, WAYNE ENTERPRISES -- NIGHT

Lucius Fox looks up as the console CHIMES.

>   FOX
>   I'm zeroing in.

>   *THE JOKER* (O.S.)
>   *Through the magic of diesel fuel*
>   *and ammonium nitrate, I'm ready*
>   *right now to blow you all sky high.*
>   *Anyone attempts to get off their*
>   *boat, you all die...*

>   FOX
>   His voice is on the ferry, but
>   that's not the source...

EXT. ROOFTOPS ABOVE GOTHAM -- NIGHT

Batman looks out, across the entire city skyline.

                    BATMAN
          Do you have a location on the
          Joker?

                    FOX (O.S.)
          It's west...

Batman FIRES UP the bat-pod- his cape SHRINKS into its pack
form as he PEELS OUT, ROARING into the night.

                    THE JOKER (O.S.)
          But we're going to make things a
          little more interesting than that.
          Tonight, we're going to learn a
          little bit about ourselves...

INT. GORDON HOME -- CONTINUOUS

Barbara Gordon answers the phone.

                    RAMIREZ (O.S.)
          Barbara, it's Anna Ramirez-

                    BARBARA
          Hi, Anna-

                    RAMIREZ (O.S.)
          Listen carefully, there's no time.
          Jim needs you to pack up and get
          the kids in the car right away.

                    BARBARA
          But the units outside-

                    RAMIREZ (O.S.)
          Barbara, those cops can't be
          trusted. Jim needs you away from
          them as soon as possible. I'll
          call them off for 10 minutes,
          you'll have to move fast-

                    BARBARA
          But where-

                    RAMIREZ (O.S.)
          I'm going to give you an address-
          Jim will meet you there...

EXT. MCU -- CONTINUOUS

Ramirez is holding the phone.

                    RAMIREZ
          250, 52nd street. Leave as soon as
          the patrol car pulls out.

Dent is holding a gun at Ramirez's head. She hangs up.

                    DENT
          She believe you?

Ramirez nods.

                    DENT (CONT'D)
          She trusts you. Just like Rachel
          did.

                    RAMIREZ
          I didn't know-

                    DENT
          'What they were gonna do'? You're
          the second cop to say that to me.
          What, *exactly*, did you think they
          were going to do?

                    RAMIREZ
          I'm sorry- they got me early on.
          My mother's medical bills and my-

                    DENT
          Don't!

Dent FLIPS his coin.

                    RAMIREZ
          I took a little from them- once
          they've got you, they keep you.
          I'm sorry.

Dent looks at his coin. Good side.

                    DENT
          Live to fight another day, officer.

Dent CRACKS her on the head with his gun.

INT. BRIDGE, PRISONER FERRY -- NIGHT

The Pilot [Prison Ferry] tries the radio. It's DEAD.

              PILOT [PRISON FERRY]
He killed the radio.

               THE JOKER (O.S.)
*There's no need for all of you to
die. That would be a waste. So
I've left you both a little
present.*

EXT. PENTHOUSE, PREWITT BUILDING -- NIGHT

The Joker stares out over the harbor, at the ferries.
Talking into a cell phone. Holding a detonator, with TWO
BUTTONS.

               THE JOKER
Each of you has a remote to blow up
the other boat.

INT. PASSENGER LOUNGE, PRISONER FERRY -- NIGHT

The Prisoners and Corrections Officers listen. Appalled.

               THE JOKER (O.S.)
*At midnight, I blow you all up.
If, however, one of you presses the
button, I'll let that boat live.
You choose. So who's it going to
be- Harvey Dent's most wanted
scumbag collection... or the sweet
innocent civilians?*
       (beat)
*Oh, and you might want to decide
quickly, because the people on the
other boat may not be quite so
noble.*

The Joker HANGS UP. The Pilot [Prisoner Ferry] looks down
at the remote in his hands. Prisoners begin YELLING and
PUSHING. The WARDEN takes the remote from the Pilot- COCKS
his shotgun. His men level their weapons at the crowd.

EXT. FERRY TERMINAL -- CONTINUOUS

Gordon looks out at the ferries. His phone rings.

               BATMAN (O.S.)
I have the Joker's location-

EXT. GOTHAM STREETS -- CONTINUOUS

Batman ROARS along on the bat-pod.

                    BATMAN
          Prewitt building. Assemble on the
          building opposite.

INT. PASSENGER LOUNGE, COMMUTER FERRY -- NIGHT

The National Guard Commander is holding the remote.
Several passengers take a step towards him. He PULLS his
weapon.

                    NATIONAL GUARD COMMANDER
          Stay back.

A BUSINESSMAN clutching his briefcase speaks up.

                    BUSINESSMAN
          Who are you to decide? We ought to
          talk it over, at least.

Other passengers agree. A MOTHER with two KIDS speaks up.

                    MOTHER
          We don't all have to die. Why
          should my babies die? Those men
          had their chance-

                    NATIONAL GUARD COMMANDER
          We're not talking about this...

                    PASSENGER 1
          They're talking over the same exact
          thing on the other boat.

                    PASSENGER 2
          If they're even bothering to talk.
          Let's put it to a vote.

INT. PASSENGER LOUNGE, PRISONER FERRY -- NIGHT

As the Prisoners grow angrier, a CORRECTIONS OFFICER FIRES
his shotgun into the air. The Prisoners back off.
Slightly.

INT. PASSENGER LOUNGE, COMMUTER FERRY -- NIGHT

A GUARDSMAN on this boat passes around a hat. People drop
CHITS into it. Passengers filling out chits eye each
other. People on their phones say goodbye to loved ones.

The Pilot [Passenger Ferry] looks out across the water to
the other Ferry. Looks up at the clock. Ten to
midnight... STARES down at his blank chit.

EXT. ROOFTOP OVERLOOKING PREWITT BUILDING -- NIGHT

Gordon and his SWAT team leaders set up SNIPER and SCOPE
positions on the balustrade.

INT. GARAGE, PREWITT BUILDING -- CONTINUOUS

A SWAT stands beside the empty school bus.

                    SWAT (INTO RADIO)
              We've found our missing bus.

EXT. ROOFTOP OVERLOOKING PREWITT BUILDING -- CONTINUOUS

Gordon looks at the SWAT LEADER.

                    GORDON
              Then we have a hostage situation.

They look across at the large windows of the Prewitt
Building. The Joker's men, in crude, homemade CLOWN MASKS
are clearly visible, automatic weapons in hand.

                    SWAT SNIPER
              I got hostages!

They look through his scope. Crouched deeper in the room,
PATIENTS, DOCTORS, and NURSES, huddled.

                    GORDON
              It's a shooting gallery. Why'd he
              choose a spot with such big
              windows?

                    BATMAN (O.S.)
              He likes the view.

Batman gestures towards the view of the ferries.

                    SWAT LEADER
              We have clear shots on five clowns.
              Snipers take them out, smash the
              windows- a team rappels in, a team
              moves in by the stairwells. 2 or 3
              or three casualties, max.

                    GORDON
               (barely hesitates)
          Let's do it.

                    BATMAN
          It's not that simple. With the
          Joker, it never is.

                    GORDON
          What's *simple*, is that every second
          we don't take him, those people on

                    GORDON
          the ferries get closer to blowing
          each other up!

                    BATMAN
          That won't happen.

                    GORDON
          Then he'll blow them both up!
          There's no time- we have to go in
          now-

                    BATMAN
          There's *always* a catch with him-

                    GORDON
          That's why we can't wait- we can't
          play his games-

Batman turns.

                    BATMAN
          I need five minutes. Alone-

                    GORDON
          No. There's no time. We have
          clear shots.

Gordon pulls his gun. Batman turns back. The SWATS watch.

                    GORDON (CONT'D)
          Dent's in there with them. We have
          to save Dent! *I* have to save Dent!
               (to SWAT Leader)
          Get ready-

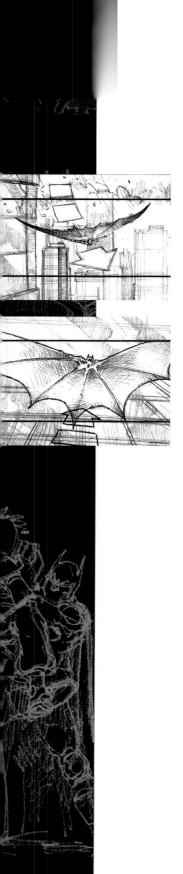

Batman LEAPS from the building, OPENS his cape- SOARS across the gulf between the two buildings- Gordon puts his weapon away. Curses softly. Turns to the SWAT leader.

>   GORDON (CONT'D)
>   Two minutes. Then you breach.

EXT. PREWITT BUILDING -- CONTINUOUS

Batman LANDS against the glass two floors below-

>   BATMAN
>   Fox. I need picture.

INT. LAB, RESEARCH AND DEVELOPMENT -- CONTINUOUS

Fox hits some keys-

>   FOX
>   You've got p.o.v. on alpha channel,
>   omni on beta-

EXT. PREWITT BUILDING -- CONTINUOUS

SMOKED GLASS EYEPIECES slip down over Batman's eye holes. *Batman's SONAR P.O.V.: the layers of the building dissolve, levels of TRANSPARENCY PULSING rhythmically... Batman can see the people inside the building...*

INT. PENTHOUSE, PREWITT BUILDING -- NIGHT

The Joker is standing by the window, looking out at his handiwork. The Chechen's DOGS start BARKING. He SMILES.

EXT. PENTHOUSE, PREWITT BUILDING -- CONTINUOUS

Batman reaches into his utility belt, SPRAYS PLASTIC onto the glass- lets it harden- PUNCHES the window-which BREAKS QUIETLY as the pieces stick to the laminate- he slips inside-

INT. PENTHOUSE, PREWITT BUILDING -- CONTINUOUS

Batman's eyes glow white as he uses his sonar to look THROUGH the corner: *AN ARMED CLOWN IS LEANING AGAINST THE CORNER...*

EXT. ROOFTOP, PREWITT BUILDING -- CONTINUOUS

A six man SWAT team prepares to rappel from the roof.

INT. STAIRWELL, PREWITT BUILDING -- CONTINUOUS

A SWAT team moves up the stairs.

EXT. ROOFTOP OVERLOOKING PREWITT BUILDING -- CONTINUOUS

Gordon's phone rings.

                  GORDON
        Hello? Barbara, calm down-

                  DENT (O.S.)
        Hello, Jim.

                  GORDON
        Harvey? What the hell's going on?

                  DENT (O.S.)
        You're about to know what my
        suffering is really like...

Gordon looks across at the Prewitt penthouse...

                  GORDON
        Where are you? Where's my family?!

                  DENT (O.S.)
        Where *my* family died.

Click. Gordon looks at the SWAT leader. Pale.

                SWAT LEADER (INTO RADIO)
        Red Team. Go!

Gordon moves to the door off the roof.

INT. PENTHOUSE, PREWITT BUILDING -- CONTINUOUS

Batman GRABS the Armed Clown, drops him, silently. He goes
to disarm him- THE WEAPON IS DUCT-TAPED TO THE CLOWN'S
HANDS. Batman RIPS off the clown mask:

STARING, FRIGHTENED EYES- MOUTH DUCT-TAPED SHUT... it's
ENGEL.

Batman looks up: Four more clowns line the windows, weapons
duct-taped to their hands. On SONAR: *he looks into where*
the hostages are crouched... the "PATIENTS" and "DOCTORS"
are carrying weapons- **these are the Joker's men...** *Above*

them SWATS RAPPEL FROM THE ROOFTOP. In the stairwells, two more teams prepping.

                    BATMAN
          Don't. Move.

Engel nods, terrified.

EXT. ROOFTOP OVERLOOKING PREWITT BUILDING -- CONTINUOUS

The SWATS line up the clowns in their sights...

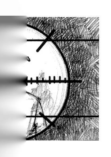

INT. STAIRWELL, PREWITT BUILDING -- CONTINUOUS

The SWAT team arrives at the penthouse fire exit. They spread CHARGES across the inner wall-

OMITTED

EXT. ROOFTOP OVERLOOKING PREWITT BUILDING -- CONTINUOUS

The SWAT Leader checks his watch.

                    SWAT LEADER (INTO RADIO)
          Go! Go! Go!

A SWAT Sniper zeroes in on a clown- the clown DISAPPEARS- the Sniper looks up, confused-

INT. PENTHOUSE, PREWITT BUILDING -- CONTINUOUS

Batman yanks the clown along the floor using his grapple gun- the clown takes down the two next to him- Batman leaps for the nearest two as SHOTS SHATTER the glass-

EXT. PREWITT BUILDING -- CONTINUOUS

The SWATS rappel down the building- SWING in through the broken windows-

INT. PENTHOUSE, PREWITT BUILDING -- CONTINUOUS

The "hostages" reel from the BLAST- The SWATS SWOOP in- aiming weapons at the clowns, throwing PERCUSSION GRENADES- Batman takes out the SWATS with fists and BATARANGS-

The last SWAT aims at BATMAN- behind him a "DOCTOR" raises a shotgun... behind the "Doctor" Batman can see through the wall at SWATS preparing to breach... Batman VAULTS over the SWAT into a two-foot kick into the "Doctor's" chest-

INT. STAIRWELL, PREWITT BUILDING -- CONTINUOUS

The Swats BLAST OUT THE WALL- the team leader steps up to
the hole... the BAT-GRAPPLE FIRES out-lodging in his kevlar
vest... he is YANKED, SCREAMING, through the door. The
rest of his team look at each other. Steel themselves.
Move in through the hole...

INT. PENTHOUSE, PREWITT BUILDING -- CONTINUOUS

As the SWATS race in they find Engel, terrified, next to a
pile of unconscious "hostages", and their team leader, one
end of an absailing rope tied around his waist. Batman is
on them, weaving KICKING, PUNCHING, and, with one hand,
clipping carabinners looped to the absailing rope onto
their webbing of vests.

Batman steps back- picks up the team leader- SWAT weapons
aim at him- he hurls the Team Leader out the window... the
SWATS watch him go... the rope pays out... one by one they
are YANKED out of the window...

EXT. ROOFTOP OVERLOOKING PREWITT BUILDING -- CONTINUOUS

A SNIPER watches through his scope as the six man SWAT team
soars out of the window and drops. The line snaps taut and
they hang, like a mountaineering team in crisis. Batman,
crouched in the broken window, secures the line.

                    SNIPER
          What the hell's he doing?

Batman looks right at the sniper- Raises his grapple gun-
BAM. The bat grapple smashes into the Sniper's scope- the
rifle is YANKED out of his hands.

INT. PREWITT BUILDING -- CONTINUOUS

Batman races past a dazed Engel...

                    ENGEL
               (pathetic)
          Thanks.

...into the main office. The Joker is there.

                    THE JOKER
          You came. I'm touched.

                    BATMAN

Where's the detonator?

The Dogs LEAP at Batman- SMASH him to the ground...

INT. PASSENGER LOUNGE, COMMUTER FERRY -- NIGHT

The Pilot [Passenger Ferry] finishes counting the votes.
Reads the verdict.

     PILOT [PASSENGER FERRY]
  The tally is 196 votes against.
   (looks down)
  And 340 votes for.

The passengers avoid eye contact with each other.

INT. PASSENGER LOUNGE, PRISONER FERRY -- NIGHT

The Corrections Officers are in a phalanx in the corner,
facing off against hundreds of menacing Prisoners.

     PRISONER 1
  Do *you* wanna die!

The Warden and his men look at each other. At the clock.

INT. PENTHOUSE, PREWITT BUILDING -- NIGHT

Batman WRESTLES with the Rotweilers- a blinding mass of
Batman, black fur and bared teeth-

The Joker POPS a switchblade. Moves in to the mass- Batman
KICKS OFF the last of the dogs- the Joker JABS his knife
into Batman's RIBS-

     THE JOKER
  All the old familiar places.

Batman recoils in pain. The Joker BUTTS him- KNEES him-
ENERGY explodes from his lean frame- he KICKS the injured
Batman back towards the glass...

INT. PASSENGER LOUNGE, COMMUTER FERRY -- NIGHT

The Pilot [Passenger Ferry] looks at the remote in his
hands.

     PILOT [PASSENGER FERRY]

> I voted for it. Same as most of
> you. Doesn't seem right that we
> should all die...

Someone calls out from the back.

> PASSENGER 3
> So do it!

> PILOT [PASSENGER FERRY]
> I didn't say *I'd* do it. Don't
> forget. We're still here. Which
> means they haven't killed us, yet,
> either.

He sets the remote down on a bench in the front of the
lounge. The other passengers and guardsmen stare at it...

INT. PASSENGER LOUNGE, PRISONER FERRY -- NIGHT

A HUGE, TATTOOED PRISONER pushes his way to the front. He
walks towards the Warden, who is sweating, looking at the
remote.

> TATTOOED PRISONER
> You don't wanna die. But you don't
> know how to take a life. Give it
> to me.

The Warden looks at the remote. At the clock.

> TATTOOED PRISONER (CONT'D)
> These men will kill you and take
> it, anyway. Give it to me, you can
> tell people I took it by force...
> give it to me and I'll do what you
> should have done ten minutes ago.

INT. PASSENGER LOUNGE, COMMUTER FERRY -- NIGHT

Everyone stares at the remote. One minute left. The
Businessman stands. Walks over and picks it up.

> BUSINESSMAN
> No one wants to get their hands
> dirty. Fine. I'll do it. Those
> men on that boat made their
> choices. They chose to murder and
> steal. It makes no sense for us to
> die, too.

He looks at the other passengers. No one makes eye
contact.

INT. PASSENGER LOUNGE, PRISONER FERRY -- NIGHT

The Warden slowly hands him the REMOTE. The Prisoner looks
at it. He looks the Warden in the eye...

Then TOSSES the remote out the window.

Warden, prisoners and officers are stunned.

EXT. PENTHOUSE, PREWITT BUILDING -- NIGHT

Batman FLIES backwards THROUGH THE WINDOW- glass flying-
the Joker KICKS out a wooden brace holding up the STEEL
FRAME- Batman's arms fly up as it comes crashing down onto
his neck- saved by his protective gauntlets. Batman GRUNTS
as the Joker STEPS onto the steel beam...

                    THE JOKER
               If we don't stop fighting, we're
               going to miss the fireworks.

                    BATMAN
               There won't *be* any fireworks.

Batman STRUGGLES to keep the beam from CRUSHING his neck...

INT. PASSENGER LOUNGE, COMMUTER FERRY -- NIGHT

The Businessman stares at the remote in his hands.
Finally, he puts it down. Sits down. Waits to die.

The clock strikes MIDNIGHT.

EXT. PENTHOUSE, PREWITT BUILDING -- NIGHT

Batman indicates the clock... twelve o'clock.

                    BATMAN
               What were you hoping to prove?
               That deep down, we're all as ugly
               as you?

The Joker looks at the clock...

INT. BOTH FERRIES -- CONTINUOUS

The Passengers brace. Look at the clock. Confused...

INT. PREWITT BUILDING -- CONTINUOUS

The smile disappears from the Joker's face.

                    BATMAN
          You're alone.

The Joker CROUCHES down, hovering above Batman's face and
arms. Shows him the remote.

                    THE JOKER
          Can't rely on anyone these days.

The Joker ARMS the remote...

                    THE JOKER (CONT'D)
          Have to do everything yourself. I
          always have- and it's not always
          easy...

                    THE JOKER
               (smiles,
                remembering)
          You know how I got these scars?

Batman looks up at him.

                    BATMAN
          No. But I know how you get *these*-

Batman's SCALLOP BLADES FIRE OUT OF HIS GAUNTLET, nailing
the Joker in the chest and arm- he STAGGERS back- Batman,
freed, leaps forward- KICKS HIM OVER THE EDGE- GRABS the
remote-

The Joker GIGGLES as he FALLS, enjoying the ride.
Something SLAMS into his leg, and he JERKS to a stop-
BATMAN'S GRAPPLE. The Joker HOLLERS in pain as Batman
HAULS him up.

                    THE JOKER
          Just couldn't let me go, could you?
          I guess this is what happens when
          an unstoppable force meets an
          immovable object. You truly are
          incorruptible, aren't you?

Batman secures the Joker UPSIDE DOWN. The Joker is
LAUGHING.

                    THE JOKER (CONT'D)
          You won't kill *me* out of some
          misplaced sense of self-
          righteousness... and *I* won't kill
          you because you're too much fun.
          We're going to do this forever.

                    BATMAN
          You'll be in a padded cell,
          forever.

                    THE JOKER
          Maybe we can share it. They'll
          need to double up, the rate this
          city's inhabitants are losing their
          minds...

                    BATMAN
          This city just showed you it's full
          of people ready to believe in *good*.

The Joker looks up at him. A twinkle in his eye.

                    THE JOKER
          Till their spirit breaks
          completely. Until they find out
          what I did with the best of them.
          Until they get a good look at the
          real Harvey Dent, and all the
          heroic things he's done.
                    (indicates ferry)
          Then those criminals will be
          straight back onto the streets and
          Gotham will understand the true
          nature of heroism.

                    THE JOKER
                    (off look)
          You didn't think I'd risk losing
          the battle for the soul of Gotham
          in a fist fight with you? You've
          got to have an ace in the hole.
          Mine's Harvey.

Batman hauls the Joker up, nose to nose.

                    BATMAN
          What did you do?

229

                        THE JOKER
          I took Gotham's white knight. And
          I brought him down to my level. It
          wasn't hard- madness is like
          gravity. All it takes is a little
          push.

Joker laughs. Batman leaves him to the SWATS.

                        BATMAN
          Lucius. Find Harvey Dent.

EXT. BURNT WAREHOUSE, 52ND STREET -- NIGHT

Gordon gets out of his car, gun drawn. Makes his way into
the blackened wreck of a building...

INT. BURNT WAREHOUSE, 52ND STREET -- NIGHT

Gordon peers into the darkness.

                        GORDON
          Dent?

No reply. Gordon makes his way deeper. Up the stairs.

INT. SECOND FLOOR, BURNT WAREHOUSE -- NIGHT

Gordon spots Barbara and their two children huddled
together. He moves towards them- Barbara is shaking her
head-

WHAM! Dent cracks Gordon over the head with his gun. Dent
disarms Gordon, rolls him over. He turns to look at the
ENORMOUS hole in the floor. From this side, in the
moonlight, Dent looks completely normal.

                        DENT
          This is where they brought her,
          Gordon. After your people handed
          her over. This is where they bound
          her. This is where she suffered.
          This is where she died.

                        GORDON
          I know. I was here. Trying to
          save her.

Dent TURNS, revealing his dark side.

                    DENT
          But you didn't, did you?

                    GORDON
          I couldn't.

                    DENT
          Yes, you could.

                    DENT
          If you'd listened to me- if you'd
          stood up against corruption instead
          of doing your deal with the devil.

                    GORDON
          I was trying to fight the mob-

Dent MOVES towards Gordon.

                    DENT
          You wouldn't dare try to justify
          yourself if you knew what I'd lost.
          Have you ever had to talk to the
          person you love most, wondering if
          you're about to listen to them die?
          You ever had to lie to that person?
          Tell them it's going to be all
          right, when you know it's not?
          Well, you're about to find out what
          that feels like. *Then* you'll be
          able to look me in the eye and tell
          me you're sorry.

Dent turns- steps over to Barbara- puts the gun to her
temple-

                    GORDON
          Harvey. Put the gun down. You're
          not going to hurt my family.

                    DENT
          No, just the person you need most.
               (cocks gun)
          So is it your wife?

                    GORDON
          Put the gun down.

Dent moves the gun to point at Gordon's little girl.

> GORDON (CONT'D)
> Please, Harvey...

Dent moves to James Gordon. Brushes the hair out of the boy's eyes with the muzzle. Gordon SNAPS.

> GORDON (CONT'D)
> Goddamit. Stop pointing that gun
> at my family, Dent.

> DENT
> We have a winner.

Dent pulls the boy away from his mother.

> BARBARA
> No! Jim stop him! Don't let him!

Dent walks James past Gordon to the edge of the burnt floor. He touches the raw wood at the edge of the floor.

> GORDON
> I'm sorry, Harvey. For everything.
> But, please. Please don't hurt
> him.

SIRENS.

EXT. BURNT WAREHOUSE, 52ND STREET -- CONTINUOUS

Cop cars descend on the warehouse.

INT. SECOND FLOOR, BURNT WAREHOUSE -- CONTINUOUS

Dent looks at Gordon, FURIOUS.

> DENT
> You brought your *cops*?

> GORDON
> All they know is there's a
> situation. They don't know who, or
> what. They're just creating a
> perimeter.

> DENT
> You think I want to *escape*?!
> There's no *escape* from this-

Dent indicates his face. His suffering.

                    GORDON
          No one needs to escape, because no
          one's done anything wrong. And
          nobody has to.

Dent chuckles. A macabre sight.

                    DENT
          I've done plenty wrong, Gordon.
          Just not quite enough. Yet.

Dent squeezes the gun a little tighter against the little
boy's neck. The boy WHIMPERS.

                    BATMAN (O.S.)
          You don't want to hurt the boy,
          Dent.

Dent turns. Batman steps from the shadows.

                    DENT
          It's not about what I want. It's
          about what's *fair*.
               (to Gordon and
                Batman)
          You thought we could be decent men
          in an indecent world. You thought
          we could lead by example. You
          thought the rules could be bent but
          not break... you were wrong. The
          world is cruel.
               (shows his coin)
          And the only morality in a cruel
          world is chance. Unbiased.
          Unprejudiced. *Fair.*

                    BATMAN
          Nothing fair ever came out of the
          barrel of a gun, Dent.

                    DENT
               (shows the coin)
          His boy's got the same chance she
          had. Fifty-fifty.

Batman steps closer, desperate, trying to reach Dent.

                    BATMAN

> What happened to Rachel wasn't
> chance. We decided to act. We
> three. We knew the risks and we
> acted as one. We are all
> responsible for the consequences.

Dent looks at Batman. Pleading.

>   DENT
> Then why was it only me who lost
> everything?

Batman looks into Dent's eyes. Emotional.

>   BATMAN
> It wasn't.

>   DENT
>   (furious)
> The Joker chose me!

>   BATMAN
> Because you were the *best of us.*
> *He wanted to prove that even*
> *someone as good as you could fall.*

>   DENT
>   (bitter)
> And he was *right.*

>   BATMAN
> But your fooling yourself if you
> think you're letting chance decide.
> You're the one pointing the gun,
> Harvey. So point it at the people
> who were responsible. We all acted
> as one. Gordon. Me. And you.

Dent is listening, the wheels in his deranged mind turning.

>   DENT
> Fair enough.

Dent eases his grip on the boy.

>   DENT (CONT'D)
> You first.

He points the gun at Batman. FLIPS the coin. TAILS. He
SHOOTS. Batman COLLAPSES to the ground, clutching his gut.

                        DENT (CONT'D)
          My turn.

He points the gun at his own head. FLIPS the coin. HEADS.
He looks a little disappointed.

Finally, he points the gun back at Gordon's son.

                        DENT (CONT'D)
          Your turn, Gordon.

                        GORDON
          You're right, Harvey. Rachel's
          death was my fault. But punish *me*-

                        DENT
          I'm about to. Tell your son it's
          going to be all right, Gordon.
          Lie. Like I lied.

Gordon looks up. Pained. Locks eyes with his son.

                        GORDON
          It's going to be all right, son.

Dent FLIPS the coin. High. Dent's eyes FOLLOW the coin
up- Batman HURLS himself at Dent and the boy.

All three of them VANISH over the edge. A TERRIBLE CRASH-
then silence, but for the sound of DENT'S COIN, SPINNING on
the floor at the edge of the hole.

Gordon, horrified, RUNS to the edge- peers down-

Dent lies at the bottom of the hole, his neck broken.
DEAD.

The coin stops spinning, GOOD SIDE UP.

Gordon's son swings into view, HANGING from Batman, who is
holding onto a JOIST with all his strength...

Gordon reaches down to GRAB his son- HAULS him up...

Batman FALLS..., dropping and dropping, SMASHING THROUGH
protruding WOOD and PIPES... He lands HARD near Dent.

EXT. BURNT WAREHOUSE, 52ND STREET -- CONTINUOUS

The cops prepare to STORM the front door.

INT. BURNT WAREHOUSE, 52ND STREET -- CONTINUOUS

Gordon races down the stairs. Rushes over to Batman.

                    JAMES (O.S.)
          Dad, is he okay?

Gordon crouches at Batman's side. The Batman GRASPS
Gordon's arm. STAGGERS to his feet.

                    GORDON
          Thank-you.

                    BATMAN
          You don't have to-

                    GORDON
          Yes, I do.

Gordon and Batman stare down at Dent's body. Grave.

                    GORDON (CONT'D)
          The Joker won.

Gordon stares down at SCARRED SIDE of Harvey Dent.

                    GORDON (CONT'D)
          Harvey's prosecution, everything he
          fought for, everything Rachel died
          for. Undone. Whatever chance
          Gotham had of fixing itself...
          whatever chance you gave us of
          fixing our city... dies with
          Harvey's reputation. We bet it all
          on him. The Joker took the best of
          us and tore him down. People will
          lose all hope.

                    BATMAN
          No. They won't.
              (looks at Gordon)
          They can never know what he did.

                    GORDON
              (incredulous)
          Five dead? Two of them cops? We
          can't sweep that under-

                    BATMAN
          No. But the Joker cannot win.

236

Batman crouches to Dent's body.

> BATMAN (CONT'D)
> Gotham needs its true hero.

Gently, he turns Dent's head so the good side of his face is up. Gordon looks from Dent's face to Batman. Understanding.

> GORDON
> *You?* You can't-

> BATMAN
> Yes, I can.

Batman stands. Faces Gordon.

> BATMAN (CONT'D)
> You either die a hero or live long enough to see yourself become the villain. I can do those things because I'm not a hero, like Dent. *I* killed those people. That's what I can be.

> GORDON
> (angry)
> No, you can't! You're not!

Batman hands Gordon his police radio.

> BATMAN
> I'm whatever Gotham needs me to be.

INSERT CUT: GORDON STANDS AT A PODIUM AT DENT'S FUNERAL. BEHIND HIM IS A LARGE PHOTOGRAPH OF DENT SMILING.

> GORDON
> *...a hero. Not the hero we deserved- the hero we needed. Nothing less than a knight. Shining...*

> GORDON (V.O.) (CONT'D)
> They'll hunt you.

> BATMAN (V.O.)
> *You'll* hunt me.

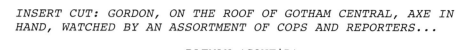

INSERT CUT: GORDON, ON THE ROOF OF GOTHAM CENTRAL, AXE IN HAND, WATCHED BY AN ASSORTMENT OF COPS AND REPORTERS...

> BATMAN (CONT'D)
> You'll condemn me, set the dogs on
> me...

GORDON TAKES THE AXE TO THE BAT SYMBOL- SPARKING, SMASHING...

> BATMAN (V.O.) (CONT'D)
> ...because it's what <u>needs</u> to
> happen.

INSERT CUT: ALFRED HOLDS THE LETTER FROM RACHEL.   THINKING.

> BATMAN (V.O.) (CONT'D)
> Because sometimes the truth isn't
> good enough...

INSERT CUT: ALFRED <u>BURNS</u> THE ENVELOPE FROM RACHEL.

> BATMAN (CONT'D)
> ...sometimes, people deserve <u>more</u>.

INSERT CUT: LUCIUS FOX TYPES HIS NAME INTO THE SONAR MACHINE.

INSERT CUT: FOX HITS THE "X". THE MACHINE FLASHES RED "SELF-DESTRUCT WARNINGS". THEN DIES. FOX SMILES TO HIMSELF.

Batman hurries off. LIMPING into the shadows.

> JAMES (O.S.)
> Batman?!

James RUNS down the stairs to join father-

> JAMES (CONT'D)
> Why's he running, Dad?!

Gordon stares after Batman.

> GORDON
> Because we have to chase him...

EXT. WAREHOUSE -- CONTINUOUS

As Cops race into the buildings the DOGS get the scent and pull away from the doorway, following the SHADOW into the stacks of shipping containers...

INT. WAREHOUSE -- CONTINUOUS

James looks at his father, confused.

> JAMES
> He didn't do anything wrong!

Gordon stares after the Batman. The sound of the dogs becoming louder and more ferocious.

> JAMES (CONT'D)
> Why, dad? Why?!

> GORDON
> Because...

EXT. DOCKSIDE ROOFTOPS -- CONTINUOUS

The Batman LURCHES between shipping containers. STUMBLING. BLEEDING. He makes it to the bat-pod...

> *GORDON* (V.O.)
> *...he's the hero Gotham deserves...*
> *but not the one it needs right now.*
> So we'll hunt him, because he can
> take it. Because he's not our
> hero...

The bat-pod streaks through Gotham's underground streets, the Batman's cape fluttering behind. A wraith...

> *GORDON* (V.O.) (CONT'D)
> *...he's a silent guardian, a*
> *watchful protector... a dark*
> *knight.*

The Batman races up a ramp into a blinding light-

CUT TO BLACK.

CREDITS.

END.

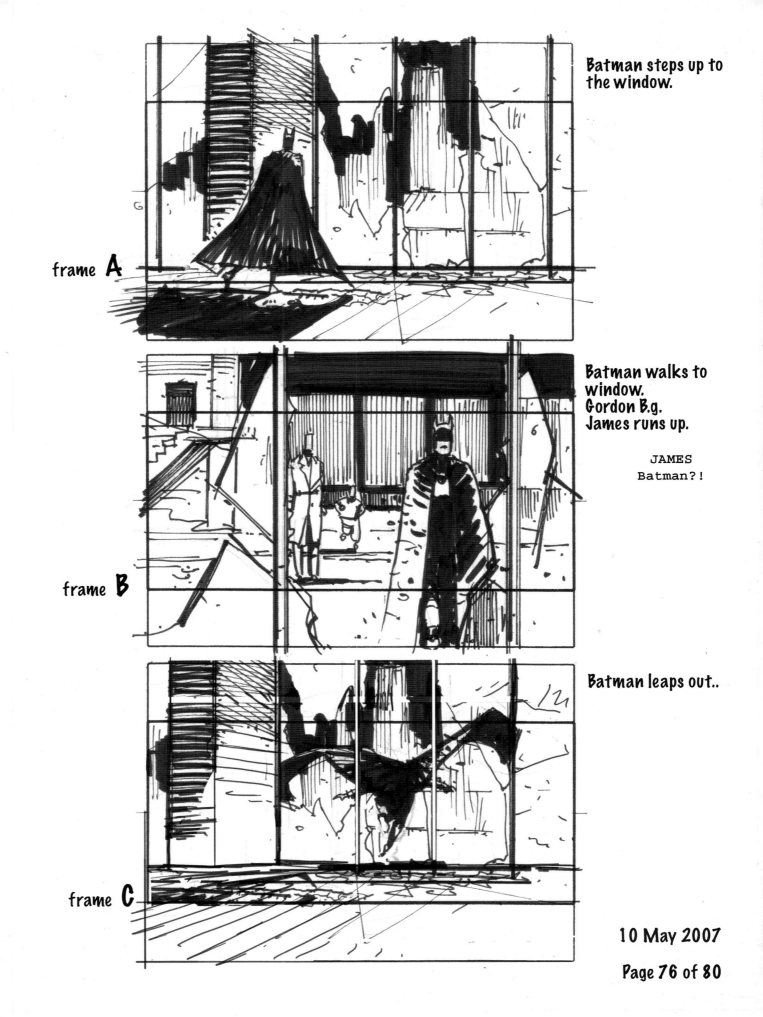

Batman steps up to
the window.

frame **A**

Batman walks to
window.
Gordon B.g.
James runs up.

JAMES
Batman?!

frame **B**

Batman leaps out..

frame **C**

10 May 2007